Talent Value Management

Endorsements

André has crafted a comprehensive and thought-provoking contribution to the still evolving discipline of talent management. He has successfully answered the challenging question of whether talent strategy drives value.

André has shifted the focus from talent administration to talent value management as a key driver in executing business strategy.

This book provides a comprehensive, well-structured, step-by-step approach to the talent value management process, supported by useful charts, tools and diagnostics.

Dave van Eeden, Author of "The role of the Chief Human Resources Officer"Executive: Organisation and People at Libstar

One thing stands out with André: It is his passion and energy and inquisitive mind. It does not surprise me he has ventured into consulting and even written a book. Also not surprising is that he has gone on to challenge the status quo around the HR way of partnering with business.

Nathan Motjuwadi, Executive: Human Resources, Capitec Bank

In this book, André not only articulates TVM as a critical enabler for successful organisations, but provides a comprehensive practical guide book on how to evolve talent administration to insightful TVM. A must-read for any business executive and HR professional tasked with organisational management and effectiveness

Ajay Dhaul, Vice President: North America Marketing Operations, Johnson and Johnson

André brings together a thought-provoking concept on how we could challenge our current practices in talent management to become more outcome-based by increasing business value while still putting the talent in the center of all decisions we make. It was great to read this thought-provoking book. I am sure you will enjoy it to!

Edwin Schenck, Senior HR leader

As a human resources executive, I have researched and read several books on talent management over many years. This is a hard-hitting book that provocatively confronts us with a major shift from contemporary talent management processes, to rethinking how talent adds value to the business and bottom line. It challenges us to move from talent administration to focusing on talent value management that liberates business growth and unlocks true business value by unleashing people's potential to deliver excellence. It's practical, loaded with tools and tips, and it is forthright. This book should be mandatory reading for all business professionals. I recommend it highly.

Professor Shirley Zinn, Group Head of Human Resources: Woolworths Holdings Ltd; and bestselling author of 'Swimming Upstream'

First published in 2017

ISBN: 978-1-86922-678-7
eISBN: 978-1-86922-679-4 (ePDF)

Published by KR Publishing
P O Box 3954
Randburg
2125
Republic of South Africa

Tel: (011) 706-6009
Fax: (011) 706-1127
E-mail: orders@knowres.co.za
Website: www.kr.co.za

Printed and bound: HartWood Digital Printing, 243 Alexandra Avenue, Halfway House, Midrand
Typesetting, layout and design: Cia Joubert, cia@knowres.co.za
Cover design: Cia Joubert, cia@knowres.co.za
Graphics designed by: Braydon Ramsden, Bonline, braydon@bonline.co.za
Editing & proofreading: Penny Abbott, pennyabbott@mweb.co.za
Project management: Cia Joubert, cia@knowres.co.za
Index created with TExtract/www.Texyz.com

Talent Value Management

Liberating Organisation Growth

by

André W. Pandy

publishing

2017

TABLE OF CONTENTS

ABOUT THE AUTHOR

André Pandy is the founder and managing director of The Human Insights Corporation, a premium boutique consultancy focusing on the formulation of impactful people solutions based on deep human and organisational insights.

He has worked in both emerging and developed markets over a 28-year period and has accumulated a wealth of insights on human and organisational dynamics in the automotive, healthcare and fast-moving consumer goods industries.

He has provided leadership at a board, senior board as well as at a global level for several of the organisations that he has worked for. These include General Motors South Africa (previously known as Delta Motor Corporation (PTY) LTD), Coca-Cola Sabco (PTY) LTD, Pioneer Foods and most recently Johnson and Johnson, where he has held several senior director roles amongst others: Senior HR Director EMEA Emerging Markets, Senior Talent Director EMEA and Senior HR Director North America Skincare.

André is adept at working in many organisational settings dealing with the most complex human and work dynamics. He is a specialist with more than 26 years of experience in HR and talent strategy formulation, coaching, change management, and creating high impact teams. His experience in the talent management space spans 19 years and he has created his own unique talent management concepts, processes and frameworks.

He is known to have created many high performing HR teams locally and internationally.

He has a B. Com (Cum Laude) from the University of the Western Cape and a B. Com (Hons) from the University of Port Elizabeth, complemented with specialised executive training at Insead – France, Ashridge University – London, and Deloitte University – Texas. He is also an internationally accredited emotional intelligence coach.

André has travelled extensively to more than 35 countries and in his spare time he does competitive road running.

ACKNOWLEDGEMENTS

To my wife Yvette and daughter Chelsea, my family and extended family for their endless support. To all my peers whose curiosity was aroused by TVM – thanks for all your input, feedback, constructive criticism, encouragements and endorsements.

PREFACE

The concept of Talent Management and its associated practices has existed for the last fifteen years and has evolved into a profession and an institution in most progressive organisations. The Human Resources function has pioneered and driven the concept and routines to ensure that organisations have sufficiently talented employees to sustain its growth.

Their tireless work has created the platform for this book.

I have been active in the Talent Management profession for more than 19 years when Talent Management was neither a profession nor a function. For us, a small team of dedicated HR professionals working for Coca-Cola Sabco (Pty) LTD, Talent Management was synonymous with the company's Mentoring programme – an extension of the Learning and Development Function.

Over the years Talent Management has morphed into a multifaceted discipline which uses multiple behavioural models, routines and frameworks. The Talent Management taxonomy contains a minimum of 12 – 15 focus areas e.g. Talent Acquisition, Talent Assessment, Talent Development and Talent Retention. All critical activities that companies use to drive the People agenda.

In today's corporate environment, most organisations will have a Head of Talent who is the custodian of an extensive Talent Strategy which has been in most cases methodically designed, but whether the outcome of the strategy drives value is another question.

Recently in a blue chip investment company, the CEO asked the Human Resources Team why they were doing Talent Management. The Team had spent endless hours preparing for the one-day session. They had all the necessary data and metrics on the current Talent pool, development plans, assessment information, performance/potential grids, pictures and short biographies of the top Talent. They had done a great administrative job – but had very little if any information on how all this added value. Their individual responses were ambiguous and confusing, as a team they were all misaligned on what and why they were doing Talent Management. Unfortunately, they are not alone – this is one of the most common challenges corporate leaders raise with me in my practice.

In another organisation I met the Head of Human Resources for the largest Division of a company which employs 36000 employees. He complained to me about spending weeks trying to extract talent data from their existing information systems so that they could formulate some insights regarding the current Talent e.g. he wanted to know how many of the female talent were recently promoted. So in this organisation Talent Management centred around data and insights (the organisation had 5 Talent Management Executives in the last 5 years!).

My conclusion and epiphany regarding Talent Management occurred to me in my last role as Senior Talent Director for a Region within Johnson and Johnson which is listed in the top 50 Fortune list – we spend far too much time on Talent Administration and far too little time on the value that the company should derive from such programmes.

It's time to review what we are doing and change our focus. Note: this does not imply that we should discard the things we are currently doing but rather shift from being administration focused to investing our time in value add activities.

It is time to evolve once again – this time starting with the business imperatives and how key Talent drive business value – Talent Value Management (TVM) is the new journey.

André Pandy
Cape Town, South Africa
April 2016

LAYOUT OF THIS BOOK

The book is divided into 5 parts – **commencing** with a basic introduction to Talent Value Management, **two middle sections** explaining the Talent Value Grid and the implementation process, and **finally a section** which looks at key TVM enablers. In total there are 14 chapters – some with more details than others.

The book is interspersed with case studies which reflect real life experiences, people and organisations. Names have been excluded for confidentiality purposes. Many illustrations and visuals are used to emphasise certain concepts. In addition, several process diagrams are included to help the reader follow the logic of the TVM sequences.

The two appendices contains a TVM diagnostic and a Talent Admin Review List.

The first part of the book is the Introduction and contains 3 chapters. **Chapter 1** provides a high level introductory overview of TVM. **Chapter 2** juxtaposes Talent Administration and Talent Value management and creates a case for change. **Chapter 3** goes deeper into the TVM philosophy, key concepts and processes.

The second part of the book has 4 chapters and contains the "core" of TVM. This section is all about the Talent Value Grid (TVG), the key tool that organisations will use to map TVM. **Chapter 4** explains what a TVG is. **Chapter 5** links business outcomes with Distinctive Internal Organisation Capabilities (DIOCs). **Chapter 6** goes deeper into the concept of Critical Roles and how they are linked to DIOCs. **Chapter 7** discusses Key Talents and how they form part of the TVG.

The third part of the book focuses on implementation of TVM and consists of 3 chapters. **Chapter 8** provides a conceptual view of the 11 step implementation process. **Chapter 9** looks at the myriad of stakeholders and their respective roles. **Chapter 10** is a concise summary of all important TVM routines.

The final part covers three TVM enablers – the things that will accelerate its impact. **Commercial Astuteness for HR** is covered as the first enabler in Chapter 11. **Chapter 12** introduces the concept and importance of Stretch Experience, **Chapter 13** presents you with useful metrics aligned to TVM and **Chapter 14** makes the case for being a TVM champion.

I trust that you will find this book thought provoking, practical and useful.

SECTION 1

THE INTRODUCTION

1

OVERVIEW: Why this book

The bottom line is that it is time for a rethink on how we do
Talent Management and the outcomes that we are trying to
achieve!

? Are you doing **Talent Administration** or are you doing **Talent Value Management (TVM)**? *This is a question that I have asked countless Chief HR Officers, Chief Talent Officers and Human Resources Professionals. The question always elicits the same response: confusion and discomfort.*

It is not that they don't understand what is being articulated, but more a conscious and at times a sub-conscious response on whether they are adding value to the organisation.

Ask a CEO the same question, and more often than not the reply would be that they are doing Talent Administration, followed by a deep curiosity on what Talent Value Management (TVM) is. With a brief succinct explanation of what TVM is all about, the CEO gets it – because it's about how Talent can drive more top and bottom line value.

? *So why as a HR Profession do we spend such an inordinate amount of time on one component of the Talent process i.e. administration?*

Should we not be spending more time on mapping what value **Key Talent** should drive and then create the Talent routines and processes to help them achieve that value? This is the realm and essence of TVM.

TVM needs to be an important and critical part of any organisation wishing to drive value with its Key Talent.

This book serves as thought leadership for HR professionals on how they can drive real value in the organisation by ensuring that there is a greater alignment of the Talent agenda to the key business outcomes – revenue, margins, cost reduction and market share.

Note: throughout this book, business outcomes will refer to revenue, margins, cost reduction and market share. In certain instances, there might be other outcomes e.g. increases in productivity and efficiency. However in the TVM philosophy, the first priority is always alignment to the revenue, margins, cost reduction and market share.

In certain not for profit organisations, the same philosophy can apply – Talent drive value, - value as defined by the specific organisation.

It can be used in Government as well as Non-Government Organisations (NGOs). The key difference will be the specific outcome that the organisation is trying to drive. For Government organisations it will for example, be cost reduction or an increase in efficiency or productivity. It will all depend what the organisation is trying to achieve.

The key challenge

Drawing the link between an organisation's Talent agenda and the value that it should drive is not an easy task as it requires:

1. Being highly commercially astute with good practical knowledge on how the company makes money. Having an understanding of key business and financial concepts and how these align with the People agenda.

2. Being able to influence key stakeholders on a new way of doing Talent Management. This introduction could be uncomfortable to an organisation given that it might discredit the current Talent

practices to which line leaders have become accustomed. The Human Resources function introduced Talent Administration to the organisation including activities such as training line leaders to use the Performance/Potential grid or how to complete a succession template.

3. Going through a rigorous process to validate who the Key Talents are that drive real value – this internal alignment on who these employees are is in itself an essential but time consuming activity. The concept of *Key Talent* will be introduced in more detail in this book.

4. A significant amount of time needs to be allocated to educating the Senior Leadership Team and other stakeholders on why there is a major shift in the Talent agenda. In a recent implementation of the TVM process in an organisation, the Head of Human Resources indicated that the concept and process was well accepted by the Executive team but he indicated that they would need at least 2 TVM cycles to truly understand how it works.

5. Patience – this is not a once-off quick fix initiative, but a comprehensive process which ensures that the organisation derives value from it.

Talent Value Management defined

TVM is a philosophy and process which ensures that Key Talents drive Distinctive Internal Organisation Capabilities which accelerate the achievement of certain business outcomes.

From the definition the following can be concluded:

- TVM becomes a philosophy or a way that an organisation does business.

- TVM is a process and not a destination.

- Distinctive Internal Organisation Capabilities (DIOCs) are an important part linking Key Talent to business outcomes. Distinctive Internal Organisation Capabilities are the collective things that an organisation does to give it a competitive advantage. It is those particular internal activities and actions that are unique to that organisation. This will be discussed in greater detail in this book.

- The Key Talents will be accountable for creating, refining or growing the Distinctive Internal Organisational Capabilities (DIOCs) – these Organisational Capabilities are the key enablers of the Business Strategy. Examples of Distinctive Internal Organisation Capabilities include: Brand Building, Third Party Distributor Management, Digital Marketing, Revenue Growth Management, Distribution Efficiency, Regulatory and Compliance Management, Government Relations. In Government or NGOs, they might include: Monitoring and Evaluation or Efficient Administration. Companies like The Coca-Cola Company will have a Brand Building DIOC at its core.

- The focus is on *Key* Talents and not the entire Talent pool of the organisation. *Key* Talents are those employees that have been selected and ratified by the organisation to drive a larger portion of value. These Talents normally form a small portion of the Talent pool.

- Business outcomes that are quantifiable.

The definition focuses on two key activities:

1. How much value is the Talent Agenda within your organisation driving? And is this value quantifiable?

2. The second component of the definition is the amount of quality time and effort that HR spends on supporting, assisting and enabling Key Talent in realising that value

? Is this not what the CEO and CFO want?

> I recently discussed the conventional Talent Management process with a very experienced Chief Financial Officer. My aim was to get a view on TVM – other than from a HR Professional. I showed her the contemporary way that Talent Management is done. There was consensus between us that the process added very little value and that in most cases companies were "retrofitting" candidates, in other words the Talent are pre-selected and then we are trying to justify how they should add value. When the TVM process was shown to her she immediately related to how it could drive business value.

In most organisations, Talent metrics are centred around lag indicators, for example, how many Talent were developed, what is the diversity profile of the Talent, what is the Talent retention rate etc. There are very few organisations that have lead indicators which draw a direct link between a Talent and what value he/she has added.

This is part of the challenge that we face today – our metrics are somewhat dated and have little or no bearing to added value. Key indicators of TVM will be discussed in a later chapter.

Note: a company can choose to use the TVM principle across the organisation – Talent must increase value, however introducing TVM expeditiously will require a top down approach – once the first strata of Talent are mapped to value then the next strata can be addressed. The case study below illustrates the point.

> I recently consulted to a major organisation which had about ten thousand employees. Of these, there was a Talent pool of approximately one thousand employees. To implement TVM across the organisation would have been a major challenge as the Executives and leaders of the organisation were still coming to grips with its concepts, principles and processes.

> When we applied the rigorous TVM process, approximately 20 Key Talents were identified to drive certain organisation capabilities which were linked to certain business outcomes. It was much easier to focus attention on those 20 Key Talents than the 1 000 people in the Talent pool.

The Key questions

TVM answers 6 questions:

1. What business outcomes are we trying to achieve?

2. What are the Distinctive Internal Critical Organisation Capabilities(DIOCs) that will help us achieve the business outcomes?

3. Which are our most Critical Roles – those which will drive the DIOCs?

4. Who are our Key Talents in those Critical Roles?

5. What is the value that these Key Talents should deliver?

6. How do we as an organisation assist these Key Talents to achieve the value?

Each of these questions will be addressed comprehensively in this book with practical examples and ideas that I have successfully used in many situations. TVM will shift your Talent activities away from Talent Administration to how you support the Key Talent in adding more value.

Why you should implement TVM

The current Talent Management processes and principles have served organisations well and have assisted them in elevating the importance of having the right people in the right roles. However, not much new thinking in a continuously changing world has emerged on how Talent Management should drive value.

There are several reasons why organisations should adopt TVM:

1. It accelerates the achievement of business outcomes.

2. It ensures that a strong pipeline of Talent will emerge as these Talents will be given challenging assignments which will stretch them and the organisation – in most instances in a positive way.

3. Value delivered by Key Talents is easier tracked and managed.

4. It will create the opportunity to review the administrative processes and routines that add little value.

5. TVM aligns certain HR activities to the business requirements.

2

WHY WE NEED RADICAL CHANGE:
Less administration and more value management

*Executive Summary: As an HR Community we are spending far too much of our time on administrative compliance and employee relations issues which add very little to an organisation's bottom line. It is now time to understand what the important levers are that make organisations successful. The focus on Key Talent driving business outcomes is an area that has been neglected as the HR function has been caught up in what it "traditionally" does in the Talent function – maintaining a process whose outcomes have become outdated and misaligned with what organisations and Talent require. Reverse engineering the Talent function starting with the business in mind and then creating the Talent processes will lead to a greater focus on value added activities. Doing it this way will increase the HR Professionals' legitimacy. Currently there is too much administration and too little **Talent Value Management.***

Our greatest HR challenge – adding value and remaining relevant to the organisation – the only way to maintain or enhance our legitimacy!

In the last 5 years many thought leaders, (individuals and organisations) have written about the HR Function and its Professionals. Unfortunately, these books and articles have been more negative than positive and have made HR appear less legitimate than other functions. Recently some positive reviews have appeared but these focus on **what** the HR function should be doing but do not provide a great amount of detail on **how**.

A review on current perspectives of where the HR function is in terms of being a value adding function reveals that there is no one specific solution to the problem. Each HR opinion leader has his/her own view and solutions on solving some of the legitimacy challenges with very little common theme on what the ultimate solution could be. Many organisations are trying to re-engineer their HR function, some with success, other less so as they are dealing with a complex challenge. I believe that it all starts with a very deep understanding of what the business requires, and then designing the function.

There are many adjectives that describe how the universe sees HR – I will not delve into the detail in this book – but can confidently state that if the TVM process is implemented in the organisation, it will double the HR Function's legitimacy. It will allow the HR Professionals to start with a business perspective and then design the Talent processes around the organisation's needs.

TVM versus Talent administration

So what is the difference between TVM and Talent administration?

Note: it is not that all Talent administration activities will be eliminated, but the focus and volume of administration duties will be replaced with a simpler process which cuts down on the administration burden. The TVM process requires less administration as its core is focusing on Key Talents and the value that they drive.

A case study regarding **Talent administration** emphasises this point.

I worked for a major Healthcare company which was listed in the Fortune 50. My role was Senior Talent Director for a major region. A large part of the role was very administrative intensive and by my reckoning I spent about 60% of my time on some of the following:

1. Compiling and maintaining a list of the top one hundred Talents. The spreadsheet contained data on names, job titles, performance, gender etc., and had at least 15 columns – which meant that there were 1500 variables in the spreadsheet. Data on the sheet changed often and updates occurred weekly.

2. Extracting metrics for reporting purposes – this happened on an ad hoc basis and infrequently it was a planned request as part of a Talent review. I was spending many hours filtering the data to extract insights on, for example, how many females were recently promoted who had a high performance rating.

3. Compiling slates (shortlists) for open vacancies. This happened often and it was a cut and paste exercise – taking data from the spreadsheet to a word document. All very time consuming and administration centric.

The company implemented an electronic system to capture employee data, however the system only contained more data on the talent and was not user-friendly enough to provide specific reports on Talent which would have eliminated a lot of the administration. Instead the opposite happened, the spreadsheets and the employee data base contained data which now had to be extracted but resided in 2 different places...more administrative work!

The case study only provides a microcosm of some of the administrative routines which is not unique to the company that I worked for but for many companies doing Talent Management the conventional way. As I work with more companies I see this on a regular basis.

? So how did we get to be so Talent administration centric?

To cut a long story short – it starts with the reason why the company is doing Talent Management and secondly it depends on the HR function's view on what it believes it should be doing in the Talent Management space. Many HR Functions will focus on building pipeline strength or succession planning – things which are outcomes of TVM and not inputs to TVM!

Note: *A company with an abundance of Key Talents who are building DIOCs which deliver tangible business outcomes will not have pipeline and succession issues!*

How much Talent administration are we doing?

A practical way to illustrate the contemporary challenge within the Talent Management area as it relates to administrative and other less value add activities is to review the current Talent Management Taxonomy (see Figure 1 below). The purpose of looking at the Taxonomy and the Talent Management process is to explore and identify where the excessive administrative activities are.

Talent Identification	Talent assessment	Talent ratification	Talent development	Talent placement	Talent retention
• Competency profiling • Creation of draft name list • Performance/ potential grid	• Behavioural profile • Administration of assessment instruments • Assessment reports	• Board ratification of talent • Organisational debate	• Needs identification • Programme selection • Deployment of development intervention	• Succession planning • Career planning • Risk mitigation	• Retention programmes • Compensation and benefits administration

Figure 1: Talent Management Taxonomy

Talent Admin Review List

The Taxonomy has been converted to a Talent Admin Review List –
(Appendix 2) which a company can use once it has commenced the
implementation of TVM to refine, refocus or eliminate some of the
administration. Below is an excerpt of the Talent Admin Review List
(Figure 2).

Activity	Build	Refine	Refocus	Eliminate
A talent philosophy exists				
A business aligned talent strategy exists				
Criteria for talent selection exist				
Talent selected according to agreed criteria				
Talent master list exists				
Criteria for talent selection exist				
Performance/potential grid used				
Talent master list updated monthly				
Annual talent review occurs				
Quarterly review of talent list and progress				
Quarterly talent reviews conducted				
Business outcomes identified for key talent to achieve				
Talent aligned to distinctive internal organisation capabilities				
Critical roles identified				
A talent value grid exists				

Figure 2: Talent Admin Review List

Refining, refocusing, building and eliminating administration

The Talent Admin Review List is a very useful tool which contains most of the activities contained in any Talent Management programme. The HR Team can conduct an exercise to challenge the way that they are doing Talent administration and use the tool for a deeper group dialogue. It will provide them with a chance to think deeply on what they are currently doing and how they could add more value. They should use this tool in the context of TVM.

So how do we eliminate some of the administration

There are three ways that this can be done – an organisation should implement all three:

1. Implement TVM, which has 3 variables to take care of business outcomes: DIOCs, Critical Roles and Key Talent. This will be covered later in the book in the form of a Talent Value Grid (TVG) which is a grid which captures and contains these 3 variables.

2. Implement an electronic system that will be able to provide Talent data in the required format.

3. Dedicate a person within the Talent team to streamline the Talent administrative activities by using The Talent Admin Review List (Appendix 2)

3

TALENT VALUE MANAGEMENT 101:
Philosophy, key concepts and processes

TVM

Executive Summary: A prerequisite for implementing TVM is having a Talent Philosophy which focuses on value creation. TVM has 12 key concepts and consists of a simple process which starts with the business imperatives and ends with the activities that HR need to perform to support the Key Talents to realise value. TVM presupposes that the HR Team have a high level of commercial astuteness to be able to understand the value and Talent link.

TVM Philosophy – the deep belief

At the core of TVM is the philosophy that Key Talents should drive a considerably higher proportion of tangible, prioritised value than other talented employees. "Tangible value" implies that it is quantifiable– it becomes a focus point for the organisation and once quantified, priorities can be agreed.

Organisations should not be conducting Talent Management programmes if there is no inherent organisation value – yet this practice continues worldwide!

Many organisations do not have a Talent Philosophy and this is the first challenge that needs to be addressed – there should be a deep belief system that should underpin the company's Talent Management practices. It provides the organisation and all its employees with a context of why they do Talent Management.

*The TVM Philosophy is simple - Key Talents
drive a higher portion of value!*

This value is measured and monitored and is underpinned with robust, focused activities that support the Key Talent in achieving the value.

In short the TVM philosophy will create the impetus for TVM to be introduced and needs to be in place before the equation below can be achieved:

*TVM = Talent achieving business outcomes + HR and
organisation focus on supporting the Talent to
achieve those outcomes*

Creating the TVM Philosophy

Philosophy versus Policy

Most organisations have policies and procedures that govern the way that they do Talent Management. In most cases the policy focuses on building the pipeline, succession management and occasionally on having talent to drive the business strategy – all important reasons for doing Talent Management. In addition, the policy will contain content on concepts, processes, roles and accountabilities and certain routines.

However, in many instances the policy is not guided by a consensus on the philosophy. A philosophy will ultimately guide the content of a "Governance Framework" within which TVM can be contained.

Below are some basic but simple possible Talent philosophies in the TVM context:

- Our Key Talent underpin our business growth
- Our Talent activities support Key Talent in delivering measurable business outcomes
- Talent drive profit

Below is a Talent philosophy **aligned with TVM** implemented by a progressive Fast Moving Consumer Goods organisation:

> *"To accelerate talent placement to drive critical organisational outcomes."*

? How can an organisation create a customised TVM Philosophy?

The simplest way is to have a top down and bottom up ratified process to align all important stakeholders, complemented by a basic change and communication plan on what the organisation's Talent Philosophy is.

Dialogue for accurate understanding and buy- in will be an important part of the implementation journey. A later section of the book will provide more detail on how best to do this.

Key TVM Concepts

Several concepts will be defined within the context of TVM. The reader might be familiar with the concept and some of the words, but not in the manner in which it used in TVM.

Some of the concepts will form the basis of additional chapters.

These concepts include:

1. TVM

2. TVM Diagnostic

3. Business Outcomes

4. Distinctive Internal Organisation Capability

5. Critical Roles

6. Key Talent or Most Valued Talent – MVT

7. Distinctive Internal Organisation Capability /Talent Grid

8. Talent Value Grid - TVG

9. Stretch Assignments

10. Talent Lead Indicators

11. Talent Value Management Activities

12. Talent Admin Review List

TVM

The TVM concept was introduced and explained in the Introduction but for reinforcement purposes it is repeated below:

> TVM is a philosophy and process which ensures that Key Talent drive Distinctive Internal Organisation Capabilities which accelerate the achievement of certain business outcomes.

Note: *the definition contains several words and phrases which were introduced earlier, for example Key Talent, this section will go deeper into each of these and other concepts.*

TVM Diagnostic

This is a specific tool to assist organisations to:

1. measure the degree to which they are doing TVM – measuring the gap versus an ideal.

2. assist in closing key gaps in the TVM process.

3. measure progress as they implement TVM.

A portion of the diagnostic is depicted in Figure 3 below: (see Appendix 1 for the full diagnostic)

Business stakeholder alignment	Status
CEO, CFO, CHRO aligned on talent costs (Talent Valuation)	Meets standard
Talent Value Management understood by key stakeholders	Exceptional
Stakeholder commitment to TVM	Meets standard
HR community understand Talent Value Management	Exceptional
Key talent take accountability for achieving business outcomes	Meets standard
A TVM philosophy exists	Gap/risk
Distinctive Internal Organisation Capabilities (DIOC)	**Status**
Common understanding on Distinctive Internal Organisational Capabilities	Meets standard
DIOC have been identified	Meets standard
The DIOC have been prioritised and agreed	Meets standard
There is a clear link between the DIOC and the business imperatives/outcomes	Meets standard

Figure 3: TVM Diagnostic

Business Outcomes

There are 4 potential business outcomes that can be realised by implementing TVM, namely revenue growth, increased margins, reduced costs or increased market share. The first 3 outcomes all lead directly to increased profitability, while an increase in market share can, but does not always, lead to an increase in profit.

The financial outcomes are briefly explained below. Note : depending on the nature of the organisation, concepts will be used differently, for example some companies might use the word revenue and others the word sales.

Revenue (or sales) = the organisation's volume (or quantity) of product or services sold multiplied by the price of the product or service. Also known as gross sales. Net sales = gross sales less discounts and sales incentives.

Gross profit = net sales revenue less cost of goods sold

Gross Margins (or gross contribution or gross margins) is the difference between revenue and costs of goods (the direct costs associated with making in the goods or service) sold divided by revenue ...expressed as a percentage. One of the aims of the company is to get its margins as high as possible.

Costs – all costs that a business will incur (in this context it will exclude production costs). Sometimes called the Selling and General Administration (SGA) costs.
Gross profit less all costs equals Earnings Before Interest, Tax, Depreciation and Amortisation. Also known as Management Income or Operating Profit

Market share – the share of a given market that an organisation will have, for example a share of the Beverage sector.

Most of these business outcomes are contained in the Income Statement (also called an Profit and Loss (P and L) Statement) of a company. Implementation of the TVM process pre-supposes that the members of the HR Team are familiar with the Income Statement of the company, particularly its concepts, layout and its method of interpretation.

Depending on the nature of the company, the Income Statement might have a slightly different format and wording, however the generic structure as shown below is universal.

Below is a **basic** Income Statement (also known as a Profit and Loss Statement) layout:

Revenue (or Sales)
Less: Cost of goods sold
Equals: Gross Profit
Less : SGA

Equals EBITDA (or simply profit)

TVM will impact the Revenue, Gross Profit (through increased margins) and the SGA lines.

Note: *some organisations might wish to create their own business outcomes and add other variables, for example improvements in productivity or efficiency.*

Distinctive Internal Organisational Capabilities (DIOCs)

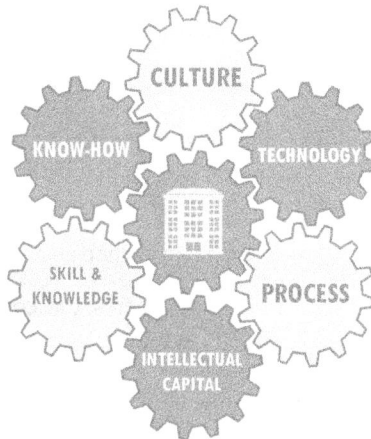

"Organisation Capabilities" is a concept which refers to a collection of business-specific activities. The term has been introduced by business authors over the last 15 years. HR Professionals should note that in this context, the term "capability" differs from the social sciences' use of the term to refer to an individual's ability or capacity to master a certain activity.

Distinctive Internal Organisational Capabilities are defined as:

> A constellation of internal organisation levers that collectively accelerates the achievement of the company's strategic imperatives and key business outcomes.

This definition is unpacked in the sections below.

Constellation of internal organisational levers

DIOCs are a collection of processes, systems or "the way we do things", which work together in a certain constellation unique to an organisation. For example: a company's unique technology combines with its culture of innovation to enable the company to create new products or services. In this example, the technology itself does not create the new products, and without the technology, the culture of innovation could not create them either. The two leverage off each other, and so we can also see DIOCs as levers.

Possible levers a company might identify (amongst others) are:

1. Company culture – for example, the way that decisions are made or the way that employees will behave when given a certain challenge.

2. Unique technology - for example, now the company uses social media platforms to expose its brands.

3. Institutionalised processes for example the process that it will use to determine customer demand.

4. Unique intellectual capital (Intellectual Property), for example, how to extract gold from a mine shaft which is five kilometres below the surface of the earth.

5. Skills and Knowledge – the unique skills and knowledge that the employees have.

Note: these levers will differ by company and will depend on a number of factors, for example, the sector within which the company operates, its product portfolio or the type of customer that it will service.

They are called **distinctive** (a company might have many internal organisation capabilities) but it is the select few that give it a competitive edge – these are the ones associated with achieving strong business results. Hence the term, Distinctive Internal Organisational Capabilities.

Additional examples of internal organisational levers:

1. The unique knowledge and skills that parts of the workforce have which are difficult to replicate e.g. knowledge of how to distribute products to consumers who are geographically remote, how to increase sales revenue using social media.

2. Technology designed exclusively for the organisation, for example sales analytics software.

3. Systems and processes designed exclusively for the organisation and employees are proficient in the use of the systems e.g. a demand planning system or a customer relationship process.

4. Company culture – the way that things are done in the organisation, the informal rules which serve as the unwritten organisation governance.

And of course the right Talent.

In most organisations there would be between **five and ten** DIOCs for example, in a Fast Moving Consumer Company one might find the following DIOCs:

- Digital marketing
- Centralised procurement
- Third party distributor management

- Sales analytics and insights

- Revenue growth management

- Brand building

- Warehouse management

There is a large number of possible DIOCs and, depending on the organisation and sector in which the company operates, the DIOCs will differ – however having the same label for the DIOC e.g. Sales analytics and insights, might be the same for 2 companies but the activities and outcomes could differ significantly.

Below is a basic case study to illustrate how talent can be used to build a DIOC:

Building Distinctive Internal Organisational Capabilities

A Healthcare organisation operating in an emerging market country had a major challenge to grow its market share. The country was highly regulated by Government on which medicinal products it could sell through traditional retail outlets and what it could sell through pharmacies. Regulation also included Government centralised price control on certain products that companies sold. To grow market share was not easy with all these local constraints. The company decided that it needed Key Talent to build this Over-The- Counter (OTC) Medicinal Organisation Capability. It eventually employed two Key Talents who were OTC experts from two different countries. Needless to say, with these Talents' effort. market share started growing and, more importantly to the company, the revenue and gross margins started to improve.

Accelerates the achievement of the company's strategic imperatives and key business outcomes

Strategic imperatives refer to the major focus areas (objectives) that a company would like to achieve in a certain time frame. The achievement of these imperatives leads to the realisation of the business outcomes.

For example, a retail bank might have Customer Service as a major strategic imperative, with the key business outcome being increased revenue through new client acquisition. In this example the DIOC might be Customer Relationship Management.

Critical Roles

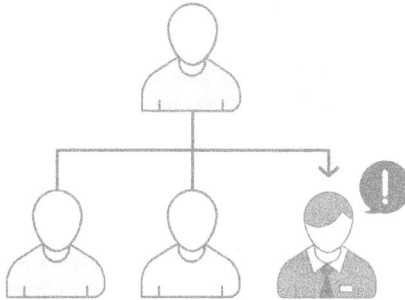

These are the roles that add a significant amount of value to the organisation and are critical to its success. TVM only focuses on those critical roles that are directly linked to a DIOC. Not that those *not* associated with organisation capabilities are not important – but it helps the company to prioritise and focus. For example, in a banking organisation, a Chief Technology Officer will be classified as a Critical Role.

A later chapter will go into greater depth on Critical Roles.

Key Talent

Key Talent (or as a friend and colleague called it – MVT – Most Valued Talent)

This differs from the generic concept of Talent or employees with potential who form part of an organisation's Talent Pool. Key Talent individuals form a sub-set of the Talent Pool and are in Critical Roles which are linked to Distinctive Internal Organisation Capabilities. In a large organisation there will not be many roles which meet these criteria.

Organisational Capability /Talent Grid

A basic grid containing information on Distinctive Internal Organisational Capabilities, Critical Roles and Key Talent (Figure 4).

This grid will eventually from part of the Talent Value Grid (defined below) which is one of the tools that organisations can use align DIOCs,Critical Roles and Key Talent. The grid can be used in three ways:

1. to record priority DIOCs;

2. to identify Critical Roles that are needed to build, refine or maintain the DIOCs;

3. to identify the Key Talents in those Critical Roles.

Capability/ business focus area and critical roles	Division 1	Division 2	Division 3	Division 4	Division 5
Brand building	Marketing executive – **Joe S**	Marketing executive – **Mark Y**	Marketing executive		
Portfolio management	Marketing managers – **Sarah X**	Marketing managers			
Consumer insights	Marketing managers				
Revenue growth management					Finance managers
Central procurement				Procurement officers	

Figure 4: DIOC Talent Grid

Talent Value Grid

A comprehensive grid that captures important information on what value the Key Talents will deliver.

Figure 5 below shows the basic headings of the grid – a subsequent chapter will go into more detail on how to build and use the grid.

Note: the first four columns in the grid contain the four business outcomes. In addition, you will notice that Key Talent data is contained in the last column. This is one of the fundamental differences in TVM.

Revenue Impact	Margin Impact	Cost Reduction Impact	Market Share Impact	Distinctive Internal Organis- ational Capability	Critical Roles	Key Talent

Figure 5: Talent Value Grid (TVG)

Stretch Experiences – "not returning to former state"

These are very specific experiences that Key Talents are given aimed to build, refine or maintain the DIOCs that will deliver the business outcome. It is about selective, focused and accurate development of the Talent in a unique and exclusive way. Each experience is explicitly linked to a DIOC.

Talent Lead Indicators

Many organisations have a myriad of Talent metrics, ranging from basic to more complex and intricate indices. In some instances, depending on the size of the organisation, an entire team will be dedicated to extracting, preparing and presenting HR and Talent information.

TVM has very specific pro-active measures which are aligned to its philosophy and process. These are called "Talent Lead Indicators" or "Talent Insights", as they give the company insights on the current state of its Talent Management activities and their alignment to business outcomes. From these insights, quick and informed decisions can be made. For example, measuring the percentage of Key Talents in Critical roles provides an immediate answer to the question: Do we have enough Key Talents in Critical Roles (by definition, these are building the DIOCs to realise certain business outcomes). If the answer to the question is negative, then it is a call to action for the HR Function to search for more Key Talent.

Talent Value Management Activities

These are the sum of all the actions that a company will engage in to start, implement and sustain TVM. A large part of the activities will be performed by the HR Function.

Talent Admin Review List (See appendix 2)

As covered in the previous chapter, this is a comprehensive list of all possible Talent activities performed by an organisation. The list can be used to streamline and eliminate unnecessary Talent administration tasks.

The Talent Value Management Process

This section will provide detail on the basic TVM process that organisations can use. Unlike the conventional Talent Management process which normally starts with a spreadsheet containing Talent names and other details, the TVM process starts with the business outcomes and ends with the Talent names.

Note: this section will only deal with the broad process and a later chapter will deal with the implementation process which will include elements of stakeholder and change management.

The TVM process is best explained in Figure 6 below:

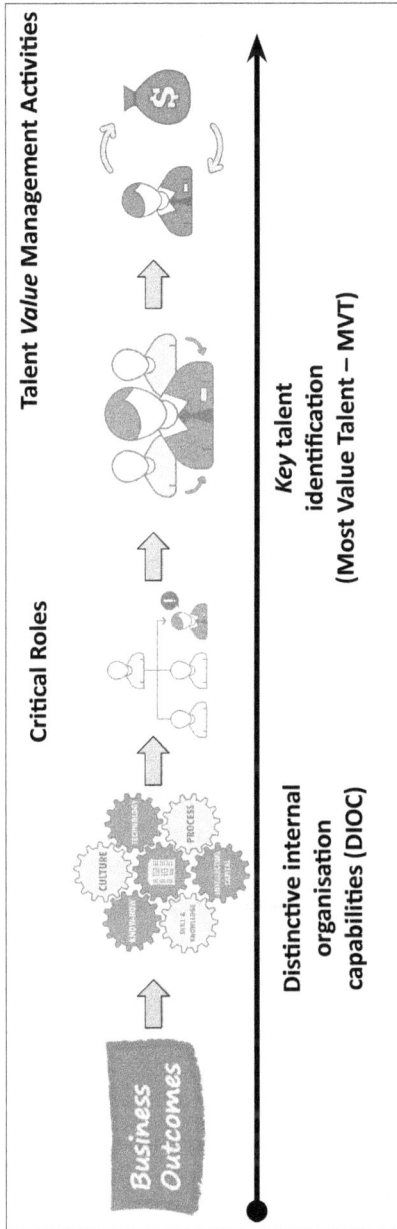

Figure 6: The TVM process

Business Outcomes – Decoding the business strategy

The first step is to review the strategic plan of the organisation, identify the key business imperatives needed to achieve the strategy for a particular period (I suggest identifying the imperatives that have to be achieved for a 12 month period, for example, it could be to launch two new products successfully). Lastly, identify what the business outcomes should be for those particular imperatives for example the launch of the two new products should bring in revenue of $ 2 million. See Figure 7 below which simplifies the strategy to business outcome steps.

Note: the initial mapping of business outcomes will provide information at an organisational level. The $ 2 million revenue that has to be achieved is the additional revenue that needs to be realised by the entire organisation. Key Talent will be mapped against a portion of that value (not necessary the whole amount). As part of the TVM process, a final review of the business outcome to be achieved by the Key Talent will be addressed.

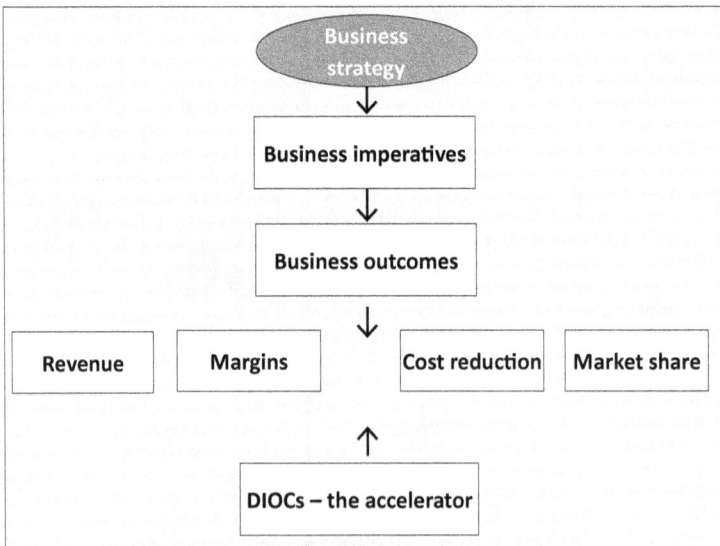

Figure 7: Linking Business Strategy to Business Outcomes

Identification of Distinctive Internal Organisational Capabilities

Many progressive companies are now starting to realise how DIOCs drive value, create competitive advantage and ignite the business strategy.
 A recent review of several companies in the Fast Moving Goods Sector indicates that they have not only identified Organisational Capabilities but have very clear plans on how they are building these. For example, Digital Marketing seems to be the latest Organisational Capability that is receiving attention – imagine how the Talent Agenda can shape this by placing the right talent to create, sustain or build the Digital Marketing Capability.

? ***The key question that needs to be asked is: Which Distinctive Internal Organisational Capabilities need to be created, refined, or maintained to achieve the identified business outcomes.***

Each of the business outcomes will be linked to a DIOC - for example the $ 2 million revenue that needs to be achieved can be linked to the Digital Marketing Capability since a large part of the plan will be to realise the additional revenue through a digital marketing strategy using various social media platforms.

Identification of Critical Roles

Not all roles in organisations are classified as critical – but all roles are important. For example, the role of the Chief Financial Officer (CFO) is more critical than that of a Finance clerk – but both are equally important. The difference is that bad judgement by a CFO can have a detrimental impact on an organisation – the consequence of error is high!

Identification of Critical Roles that are linked to the DIOCs is the next step. In a way, this provides the organisation some sort of basic audit to determine which of its roles it considers critical, using DIOCs and business outcomes as a reference point. For example, to build a Digital Marketing DIOC requires a Digital or Marketing Media Strategist as a Critical Role.

Key Talent Identification

The process of identifying and ratifying Key Talents. These are the Key Talent who are in Critical Roles. Ultimately they will have the responsibility of building, refining, maintaining or accelerating the Organisational Capabilities which will achieve the business outcomes. Note: Key Talent are a sub – set of the organisations Talent Pool – they have a larger responsibility to drive higher value.

Talent Value Management Activities

These are the specific activities that an organisation will perform to support, nurture and enable the Key Talent to realise the business outcomes. For example, to build a Digital Marketing DIOC an organisation might send a Key Talent to a highly specialised training programme on contemporary Digital Marketing practices.

SECTION 2

TALENT VALUE GRID (TVG)
STARTING WITH THE END IN MIND

INTRODUCTION

The concepts and processes within Talent Value Management can be confusing to individuals – particularly the HR team members who have been schooled to do Talent Management in a certain way.

? *What then is the simplest and most visual way to illustrate TVM?*

The answer is to look at a Talent Value Grid which was briefly introduced in the previous section. The Talent Value Grid is a basic grid which contains approximately seven important variables that are needed to map Talent to organisation value.

The grid is a culmination of methodically implementing the TVM process and filling in key information.

Section overview

Chapter 4 provides detail on all the columns within the Talent Value Grid (TVG) together with sample data to illustrate how the TVG works.

Chapter 5 will illustrate how business strategy is linked to Distinctive Internal Organisational Capabilities through the early identification of business outcomes. The business outcomes identified will be used as a selective guide to assign certain objectives for the Key Talent to achieve.

Chapter 6 will further explain how Critical Roles are linked to DIOC's. They are labelled as *Critical* as they have a direct link to the DIOC.

Chapter 7 will bring it all together and add the last column and key ingredient – the **Key Talent.** Many organisations normally start with a Talent list …unlike TVM!

4

TALENT VALUE GRID: Starting with the end in mind

Executive Summary: The TVG is a very useful tool which companies can utilise in many ways to track the progress of several Talent Management variables, for example, what value are the Talents adding; has the organisation identified which roles are critical; and does it have enough of the right Key Talent. Each column within the grid will be explained briefly in addition to how they are interconnected.

The TVG is the most useful tool to match Talent to value!

Layout of the TVG

Figure 8 below is a basic TVG grid with 7 columns (Figure 1). At this stage only the headings are depicted in the grid. In Figure 9, some sample data are inserted for illustrative purposes.

Note: *the columns are completed from left to right and mimic the TVM process which was discussed earlier.*

①	②	③	④	⑤	⑥	⑦
Revenue target	Margins target	Cost reduction target	Market share target	Distinctive internal organisational capability	Critical roles	Key talent

Figure 8: Layout of the TVG

① The revenue target appears first as this is the line item that appears at the top of a Profit and Loss statement. This is normally the first thing key stakeholders in the organisation would like to know – what is our sales target! A company can choose whether it would like to include Gross or Net Revenue (revenue after discounts and incentives have been taken into account).

② The second column contains the margins data. It could also contain the gross profit data. However, margins are a very good indicator of how cost of goods sold is being managed. Most stakeholders would be interested in the size of the margins being made.

③ The third column indicates the extent to which a company would like to reduce costs. In the first phase of creating the grid a broad cost saving number can be inserted. Note: it is better to insert the actual value that the company wishes to achieve, for example, a cost reduction of $ 300 000. Note that to reduce costs implies that most or some of the functions will contribute to the cost saving. For example, if an organisation creates a centralised procurement function then it would be expected that the Procurement function will create significant cost savings for the company. For the TVG, it is important to identify which functions are expected to contribute most of the target cost saving.

Note: *the first three columns are a reflection of the Profit and Loss statement and all the relevant data can be found in it. (whether in the budget for the coming year or the strategic plan)*

④ Market share is the fourth column. Here the organisation can insert the market share that it aspires to. Note: depending on the nature of the organisation market share might not be a prioritised business outcome. A company can substitute market share with a more relevant outcome.

⑤ Column five contains the data on the Distinctive Internal Organisational Capabilities. A company might capture between eight to ten DIOC's. Note: it will select those DIOCs which will lead to the achievement to the business outcomes in the first four columns.

⑥ Column 6 lists those roles which are directly linked to the identified DIOCs.

⑦ The last column contains the names of Key Talents that are in those identified critical roles.

Note: *the first round of completing the TVG will mostly contain data at a company level. Most likely it will be the company's targets for the year ...this company level financial and market share data will be captured in columns one to four.*

Revenue	Margins	Cost reduction	Market share	Distinctive internal organisational capability	Critical roles	Key talent
$2 million	30%	$300 000	26%	• Centralised procurement • Brand building • Distribution efficiency • Revenue growth management • Sales analytics • Category management	• Procurement manager • Marketing manager • Senior sales analyst • Distribution manager	JP PA AP CP YD

Figure 9: TVG with some sample data – first round company level data

Revenue	Margins	Cost reduction	Market share	Distinctive internal organisational capability	Critical roles	Key talent
$2 million	30%	$300 000 # $ 50,000	26%	• Centralised procurement	• Procurement manager	# JP

Figure 10: TVG with some sample data – Key Talent linked to business outcomes

You will notice that in column 3 there is a # $50 000 cost reduction target and that this will be achieved through the Centralised Procurement DIOC by the Procurement Manager. In this case JP is the Procurement manager who has been ratified as a Key Talent.

Advantages of using the TVG

The culmination of the TVM process into a TVG provides numerous benefits to the organisation. Listed below those that I deem the most important:

1. It helps to align Key Talent and business outcomes in a robust and visual manner.

2. The added benefit of identifying, building and refining DIOCs cannot be overlooked as this is key to realise the strategic objectives of the organisation.

3. It informs the company where there is a serious Talent gap - imagine that in column seven there was no Talent identified.

4. It provides crucial information on what are the most Critical Roles.

5. It creates a very visual tool which can be used periodically to track the progress of Key Talents.

5

LINKING BUSINESS OUTCOMES TO DISTINCTIVE INTERNAL ORGANISATIONAL CAPABILITIES (DIOCs):
The bridge between Key Talent and business outcomes

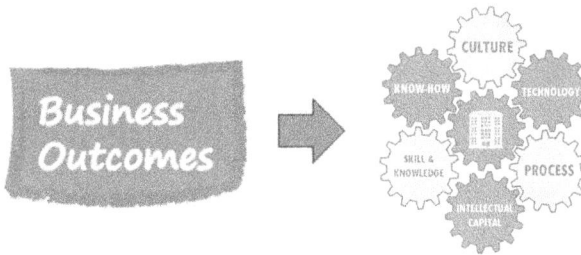

Executive Summary: Business Strategy and Strategic Imperatives are enabled by the Distinctive Internal Organisational Capabilities that an organisation has developed. These DIOCs create competitive advantage as they are normally difficult to replicate. TVM offers multiple value added business propositions for organisations. One being that Key Talents can be placed in Critical Roles that either create, refine or accelerate the DIOCs. Naturally, if the organisation has well developed DIOCs, this it should lead to the achievement of the business outcomes. Figure 11 below illustrates the point visually.

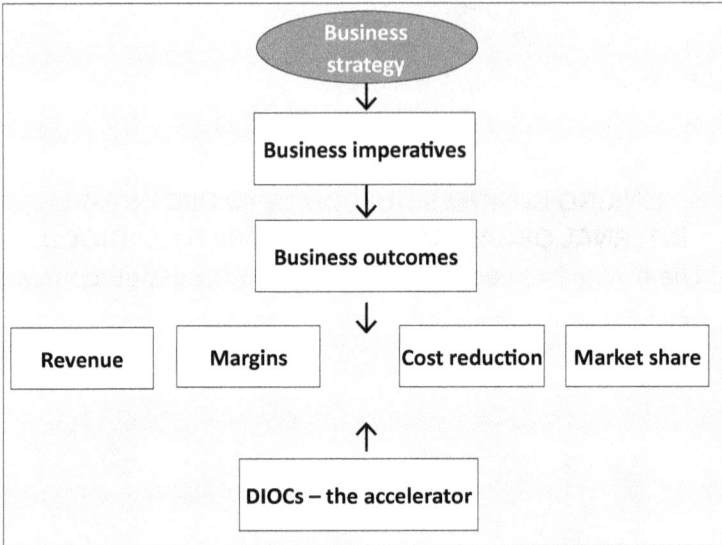

Figure 11 – Business Outcomes and DIOC link

Decoding the Business Strategy

Implementing TVM pre-supposes that a clear business strategy exists because without strategy it will be very difficult to align TVM to the business imperatives. A three-year business strategy is ideal, as it is neither too short nor too long term. Five-year business strategies are not easy to formulate and implement given the unpredictability of the external environment. A one-year strategy is more of a tactical plan – most likely linked to the annual financial plan.

Notwithstanding the nature of the company and the sector in which it operates, most strategies will focus on similar things. My experience operating at Board level has allowed me to form a mosaic of these common strategic themes:

1. Competitor analysis and how to gain market share

    a. competitor activity - new product and package launches or services
    b. market share.

2. Revenue Growth – either through:

    a. price increases or
    b. volume increase.

3. New product, package and service lines.

4. Margin Management

    a. discounts and allowances
    b. margin erosion
    c. cost of sale reduction.

5. Supply Chain efficiencies

    a. ensuring an efficient distribution system
    b. procurement management.

6. Improvement in productivity and cost reduction

    a. new technologies
    b. investment in capital

7. cost reduction.

TVM as described earlier in the book leads to the achievement of four business outcomes namely: revenue increases, margin increases, cost reduction, and an increase in market share. Depending on the business strategy, all four are possible outcomes, however a business might choose to focus on two to three – e.g. a greater emphasis on revenue and margin management (which will impact profit).

A good business strategy and a sound financial plan to underpin it will ultimately increase an organisation's profit (uncontrollable natural disasters permitting). To achieve the strategy and strategic imperatives, DIOCs need to be identified.

Distinctive Internal Organisational Capabilities (DIOCs)

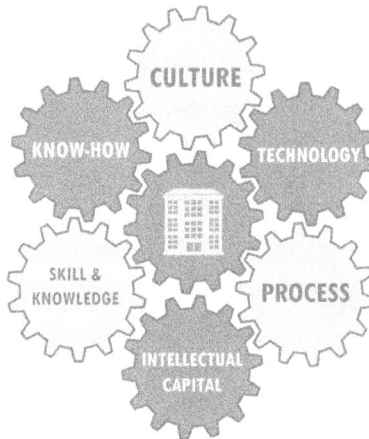

A DIOC is something that either exists, needs refinement or needs to be created in an organisation. As previously defined it is:

> A constellation of internal levers that collectively accelerates the achievement of the company's strategy, strategic imperatives and key business outcomes

The following case study illustrates how a DIOC could be created.

> A Healthcare company appointed a new Managing Director. The incumbent had been in various Vice President roles including the Vice President for Sales of a major region as well as the Vice President to service a Global Retail Customer.
>
> He was well endowed with knowledge and skills to guide a sales team. His understanding of the sales environment was exceptional and together with his analytical mind he was a highly capable Executive. He had a very challenging situation on his arrival as sales were significantly down compared to the previous 5 years. This was due mostly to unsuccessful product launches at the wrong price point.

In his first few months in the role he continuously requested sales data from the Sales Director but the data either arrived too late or it was not accurate enough for good decision making. To aggravate the situation, the current Sales Director was more proficient at customer relationships than decision making based on sales analytic insights. In fact, the sales function had a very small team consisting of 1 or 2 employees who provided passive sales data. Most of the sales data either came from the finance team or from an antiquated sales system.

In his previous role as VP servicing the Global Retail Customer the MD had learnt the hard way to have the correct data timeously. The Global Retail Customer constantly demanded data ….and it was incumbent on the Vice President to provide these as required. In addition, the Global Retailer was very strong in a *DIOC of Data Analytics and Insights.*

The MD then made a radical move and together with the Human Resource Function created a DIOC called Sales Analytics which would provide fast, accurate fact based sales information. This move formed part of a broader business strategy to drive revenue – predominantly through an increase in volume.

Building the DIOC required several initiatives including but not limited to:

- Creating a new organisational unit within the Sales function called Sales Analytics;

- Recruitment of specialists in the analytics field;

- Training and development of the analytics team as well as several other teams in other Functions e.g. the Marketing Team;

- Creating robust sales analytics routines and processes – data had to be presented in a certain way within a specified time frame e.g. monthly;

- Placing a Key Talent to oversee and manage the Sales Analytics function.

> After a year, the unit became highly proficient in providing key internal stakeholders with timeous sales information to drive business outcomes and was a major contributor to the subsequent increase in sales volume – a key strategic imperative.

The case study above details a number of key points regarding the Business Strategy and DIOC alignment:

1.   There has to be clarity on what the strategic imperatives are;

2.   The identification of DIOCs requires a clear and common understanding of the concept of organisation capabilities. From my experience it takes time for stakeholders to eventually understand what organisational capabilities are as indicated in the case study below:

> A few years ago I facilitated an annual Talent review with the Management Board (my role at the time was HR Director). As a team we had done several successful Talent reviews (success defined in the traditional Talent administration way) – but this one was going to be different – I was going to help the team identify the Distinctive Internal Organisational Capabilities that would drive the business imperatives.
>
> The team were very creative in the way the business imperatives were presented – there were five business imperatives and we used visuals of the "big five" and used the analogy of the African big five game e.g. elephant, lion, water buffalo etc., to represent each of the imperatives. This was the easy part and the Management Board was very aligned on what the five were.
>
> The challenge that arose was two-fold: first the Management Board was really not clear on what an organisational capability was and even worse, drawing the link between a business imperative and an organisational capability proved difficult. It was the first time that the team had been introduced to this concept and process.

> Needless to say after four to five hours of trying to identify and align organisational capabilities the Management Board was not clear on what was trying to be achieved.
>
> In retrospect, the process that was adopted to educate the Management Board should have started a very long time before the session.
>
> The lesson learnt was more than an alignment lesson but shows that it is important to start early in the TVM process to educate key stakeholders.
>
> Fortunately, in today's business environment there is a much better understanding of the organisational capability concept.

3. The identification of DIOCs takes place with the strategic imperatives as the back drop and requires multiple stakeholders to be involved to ensure a collective view across the organisation;

4. Each DIOC has to accelerate the achievement of a strategic imperative and must be further linked to a business outcome. For example, Sales Volume Growth is the business imperative, the business outcome is 10% growth and the DIOC that will have a direct contribution toward the achievement of the 10% is Sales Analytics.

A simple example in a grid format as in Figure 12 might create clarity on the link between DIOCs, Business Imperatives and Business outcomes:

Business Imperative	Business Outcome	Distinctive Internal Organisational Capability
Revenue increase through social media as marketing platform	*Two percent gross revenue increase for January to December*	*Digital marketing*

Figure 12 – DIOC and Business Outcome link

Lessons learnt in linking the DIOC, the Strategic Imperatives and Business Outcomes

6. A clear business strategy has to exist with supporting financial outcomes.

7. The strategy has to be broken down into imperatives.

8. Ensure adequate alignment and education on the concept of organisational capabilities and how they activate business strategy.

9. Be sure to use very simple practical examples of things that the company is already doing that reflect this process – it might just need to be explained in a sequential and logical manner.

6

LINKING BUSINESS OUTCOMES, DIOCs AND CRITICAL ROLES:
Critical roles – vital for business success

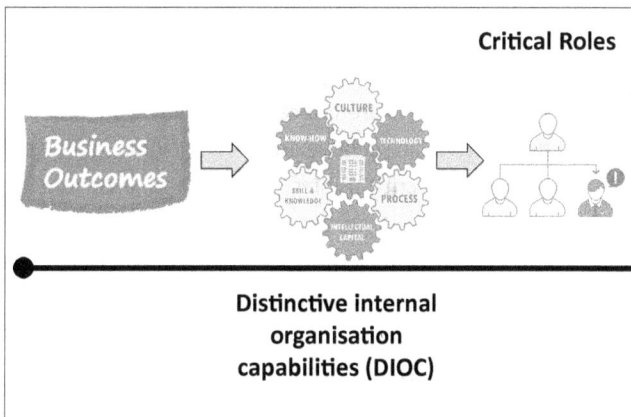

Executive Summary: *Organisations have many Critical Roles which are important and key to its success. These roles are core to what the organisation is all about or what it is trying to achieve. Within each DIOC there are a few roles which, due to their nature, are absolutely critical to "igniting" the DIOC.*

The alignment of Business Outcomes, DIOC's and Critical Roles is not a simple process as all three factors have to be considered in a logical and chronological way. One can only determine one before the other. For example business outcomes will always precede the identification of DIOCs.

Critical versus other roles

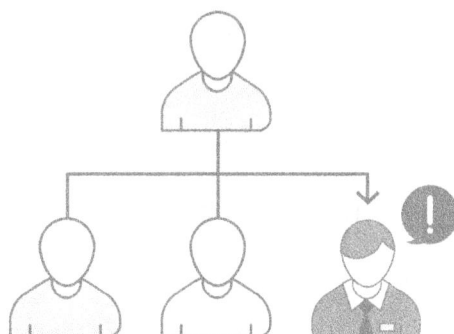

Not all roles in organisations are critical - they might be important but are not essential to drive direct value. Below is a list of eight factors that can be used to determine critical roles. These can be used as a checklist when differentiating amongst various roles and can serve as a funnel to select the top fifteen to twenty roles (the number of critical roles will depend on the size and complexity of the company).

1.   Linked to business strategy and outcomes

These roles will have (in most instances) a link to some key business outcomes. Let's continue with the example of the Distribution Manager (Critical Role) and Distribution Efficiency (the DIOC). Of the four possible business outcomes (these were articulated several times in previous chapters), Distribution Efficiency will have the most significant impact on the gross profit margin of a company. The more a company reduces its cost of distribution (fuel, maintenance and other costs), the higher the gross profit margin will be. This is a challenge that faces many companies today, particularly those operating in Emerging Market economies which have many unplanned dynamics to deal with such as fuel price fluctuations or high vehicle maintenance costs due to poor road infrastructure. It would not be a major challenge to link a tangible business outcome to Distribution Efficiency. An organisation can set a basic target e.g. reduce the maintenance cost by 5% versus the current year budget or prior year actuals by implementing a tyre management programme that will ensure that truck drivers drive in a prescribed manner.

2. Distinctive Internal Organisational Capability Link

These are the roles, in the TVM context, that are directly linked to the DIOCs. As emphasised previously, a company will have between eight to ten DIOCs. Any more will dilute the company's focus on the "distinctive" capabilities. For example, if the DIOC is Distribution Efficiency. then the Distribution Manager role is critical. Note: several roles could be linked to a DIOC; however, the selection should be on the "critical" or most important role (not necessary the most senior role). Figure 13 is an example (content modified to maintain client confidentiality) of a grid that I designed for an organisation which links DIOCs and Critical Roles:

Capability/ business focus area and critical roles	Division 1	Division 2	Division 3	Division 4	Division 5
Brand building	Marketing executive	Marketing executive	Marketing executive		
Portfolio management	Marketing managers	Marketing managers			
Consumer insights	Marketing managers				
Revenue growth management					Finance managers
Central procurement				Procurement officers	

Figure 13 : DIOC and Critical role link

3. Drive higher value

Critical roles are those that drive a higher proportion of value. By linking thes roles to DIOCs and business outcome in a logical way, it is easier to see why the role should drive a higher portion of value when compared to other roles. For example, a Distribution Manager who is driving Distribution Efficiency should add more value than a distribution or warehousing clerk. This does not undermine the other roles which all have to make a contribution, but the inherent requirements and outcomes of certain roles do drive more organisational value.

4. Difficulty of finding the necessary role holders in the job market

My experience has shown that it is not easy to find the requisite skill set in the job market for an incumbent who will occupy a critical role to drive a DIOC. The abundance of incumbents will also depend on the country, the sector and several other factors e.g. graduates in the specific profession. The secondary challenge is the required skill level and technical knowledge required for the critical role. Most critical roles require a proficient incumbent who has mastered a certain type of role over a number of years. Where it will take some time to fill a vacancy in a role which directly impacts a business outcome, this role would be considered critical for retention.

5. Evolve over time

No organisation operates in a static environment and the DIOCs that are relevant today might be less relevant in the future. Needless to say, the roles that drive the DIOC will also evolve and in some instances the critical roles today might also be less relevant in the future. The organisation has to do a reality check regularly (I suggest annually) on which critical roles will have a major impact on the organisation for the coming period. For example, in today's high tech environment, incumbents who are in roles that understand how best to use cloud technology and storage of company data might be an evolving critical role, particularly if an organisation requires a "data scientist" to extract valuable information to make fact based decision making. In this example, Business Insight generation could become a DIOC.

6.   Important to achievement of company strategy

These roles have a direct and disproportionate strategic impact on the business. The position is mission critical to the accomplishment of the strategic imperatives. The collective number of Critical Roles in an organisation must lead to the achievement of a part of the company's business strategy (if occupied by the correct incumbent). As indicated earlier, these roles drive higher value hence they are important for organisational success.

7.   Will vary by organisational job level

Not all Critical Roles are at the senior level of an organisation, however most tend to be at a level which requires good judgement and have a high consequence of error. In some instances, the role might be in a specialty function which does not need to be hierarchically high but has a major impact on the organisation's results. For example, in the Fast Moving Consumer Goods Industry, given the nature of the business sector where speed and accuracy of information on consumer trends is important for success, a Demand Planner role (normally this is a specialist role) is important to drive the Demand Planning DIOC. The level of the role is normally at a supervisory level, however the consequences of demand planning errors are high and can lead to too much or too little inventory – which will impact profitability.

8.   Are essential for succession planning

Finally, roles where a sudden exodus of incumbents in these roles with no ready successors will affect the running of the company are critical roles, particularly in smaller businesses. Ideally these roles and the succession thereof are prioritised higher than others.

The case study below describes the importance of Critical Roles.

Several years ago the organisation that I worked for experienced a major set-back when one of the incumbents in a Critical Role suddenly left the organisation on short notice. The incumbent was in a Regulatory role (a compliance type role) and was responsible for the preparation of highly technical dossiers which were submitted to the Government's Department of Health. An approved dossier would allow the company to sell certain medicinal products in a country. Dossier approval was a complex and time consuming process and required up to a year for preparation and approval. The incumbent was preparing several new submissions and was dealing directly with Health Officials in the government. When she suddenly left, all this work came to a grinding halt and there was nobody to replace her, and even worse, within the country that she operated in (it was an Eastern European country) there were very few Regulatory specialists in the job market. Proper succession planning would have avoided the crisis. The company lost $ 10 million dollars of sales as the products could not be brought to market without Government approval.

7

BRINGING IT ALL TOGETHER: Creating the TVG with Key Talent at the core

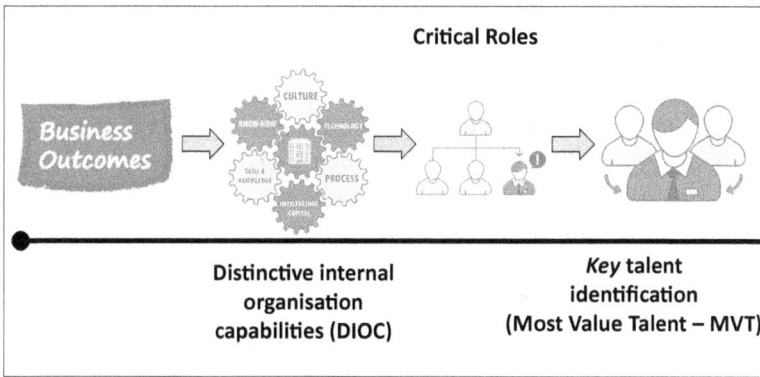

Critical Roles

Business Outcomes

Distinctive internal organisation capabilities (DIOC)

Key **talent identification (Most Value Talent – MVT)**

Executive Summary: The essence of TVM is that Talents add value! This segment will provide more detail on what is meant by Key Talent and why the fourth step in the process is the Talent list. In addition, the reason for having it as the last column in the TVG will be further emphasized. This chapter moves from the "hard" to the "soft" stuff.

So what is a Key Talent?

The Key Talents are those individuals in Critical Roles, who are able to build, sustain or enhance a DIOC and in so doing either increase quantifiable revenue, margins, and market share or decrease costs.

? *Key question: are all employees in the organisation's talent pool considered Key Talent?*

Most progressive organisations will have a talent pool or a Talent list composed of individuals who have been identified by key stakeholders as having the potential to advance in the organisation.

Figure 14 below illustrates the difference between employees in the generic Talent pool versus those that are directly linked to the DIOC. The diagram depicts 4 subsets of a fictitious organisation's Talent "universe" (a total of 370 employees). Talent pool A contains 200 employees and Talent pool D 20. Talent pool D contains the Key Talent. Note: the difference between Talent Pool A and Pool D is that the Talent in A have been identified as being in critical roles which drive the DIOCs.

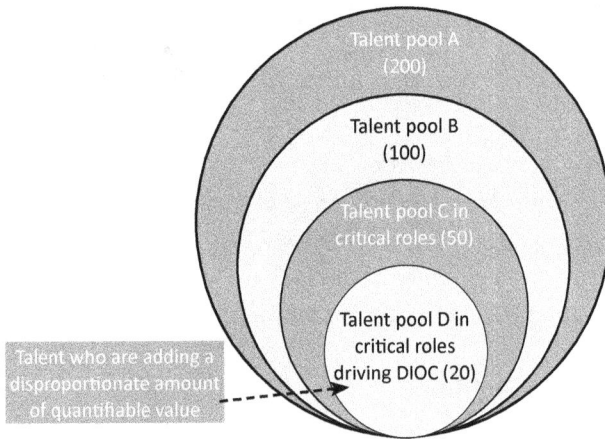

Figure 14: Talent Pools

✎ *Note: In many instances the Talent pool identification and how the Talent are utilised can be problematic. Here are some of my observations regarding this which I have accumulated over a 15-year period (TVM eliminates all these issues!) :*

Initial Talent Identification

This is normally done on an intermittent basis in the organisation with very little regard to what the key strategic imperatives are and how the Talents will achieve this. Occasionally the organisation will try and link the Talent Agenda to the Business Agenda, however there is normally a vague and weak link between the 2 – it normally ends up being an academic or theoretical exercise.

The process of initial identification of talent is normally a request for names of individuals who meet certain criteria. This exercise normally culminates in an extensive name list. I believe this is where Talent Administration begins. Imagine maintaining a large list of Talents with all their demographic and work details!

Because of the sheer size of the list, often companies will segment it and create several strata of talent. The primary focus of TVM is on the Key Talents – those who are in Critical Roles that drive the DIOC to achieve business outcomes. In most instances, it will be those roles that are "top of the house".

Political list

It seems when a list of Talents is requested from internal Functions / Business Heads this becomes a political process. Regardless of the criteria being used, they will select incumbents who are not going to drive the value that is required. Imagine a senior leader indicating that they have no Talent in their function – sounds like suicide! Hence they will come up with a name list and will try and justify why the incumbents are talent. Normally when a cycle of promotion or succession arises you will find that very few of those incumbents who were deemed to be Talent meet the criteria for the role!

TVM eliminates or mitigates these biases by focusing on a reverse engineered process but also how Key Talents are defined. Because the rigour in the process starts with the identification of the business imperative and outcomes, the DIOC, and the Critical roles, then only is there a deeper dialogue on the Talent. By the time the first 3 steps are completed, several incumbents have been eliminated and only those within the TVM context are then classified as Key Talents.

> **Note:** *It does not mean that those who were eliminated during the process are not talent – it just provides a greater focus on the Key Talents who are responsible for business growth. The other Talents will still be on a list (hopefully by then HR start to align them to some key business initiatives). Given the organisation resources allocated to Talent Management, it is not possible to TVM a few hundred incumbents in the short term!*

Key Talents still have to meet all the pre-requisite requirements that a company uses to determine who should be on a Talent list. One does not select an incumbent as a Key Talent because he/she occupies a Critical Role that drives a DIOC. In many cases, the organisation will find that the process of identifying Key Talents in Critical roles points to a larger Talent gap in the organisation, particularly when there are very few Talents in Critical Roles. A TVG normally helps the organisation's Talent gaps identification.

The TVM process will be used to identify Talent within the organisation. The key question is what happens to those Talent who are not considered as Key Talent. Those classified as "non" Key Talent are still part of the Talent Programme of the company. The difference will be the degree of attention and focus that the Key Talent will receive. It is not always possible for an organisation to focus on an entire Talent Pool in the same way as the Key Talent – it will not have the resources to do this uniformly across a large organisation (smaller companies might incorporate the whole Talent Pool as Key Talent). However – the same principle regarding Talent must add value can be used for the entire Talent pool.

The Organisational Capability /Talent Grid

As described previously, the Organisational Capability/Talent grid is a tool which can be used by organisations to map out the DIOC, Critical Role and Talent link. Figure 15 below is an example of a grid containing sample data. For example, you will notice that in Division 2, Brand Building is a DIOC and that the Marketing Executive is a Critical Role to build the DIOC. In this case the Talent's name is Mark Y.

Capability/ business focus area and critical roles	Division 1	Division 2	Division 3	Division 4	Division 5
Brand building	Marketing executive – **Joe S**	Marketing executive – **Mark Y**	Marketing executive		
Portfolio management	Marketing managers – **Sarah X**	Marketing managers			
Consumer insights	Marketing managers				
Revenue growth management					Finance managers
Central procurement				Procurement officers	

Figure 15: Organisational Capability/Talent Grid

SECTION 3

IMPLEMENTING AND SUSTAINING TVM

INTRODUCTION

This section will provide you with a step by step guide to implementing TVM but more importantly, sustaining it. TVM implementation does indeed require a basic project plan complemented by an influencing plan to address the needs and aspirations of several stakeholder groups. Key sponsors will be the CEO and CFO as TVM has a very strong business orientation. A comprehensive implementation road map is included in this section as well as some routines on sustaining TVM. The implementation process will be split into several parts from pre-deployment to final implementation.

Section overview

Chapter 8 provides a high level view of the 11 steps (the last 2 steps are covered in the final segment of the book under the TVM Accelerators heading).

Chapter 9 will look at specific stakeholders and their respective roles during the implementation and sustain phases. There will be a separate section on the role that the Human Resources Function will play.

Chapter 10 will focus on the most important routines that underpin TVM.

8

A BIRDS EYE VIEW OF THE IMPLEMENTATION PROCESS:
The 11 steps

Executive Summary: The TVM implementation process has 11 steps, 2 of which are optional. The first phase consists of diagnosis and requires some base data to create the TVM "story" within the organisation. The second phase is the creation of a Talent Philosophy in a syndicated way. Phase 3 culminates in the formulation of the TVG. The last mandatory phase is implementing routines that will sustain TVM. Two additional steps on creating stretch experiences and Talent Insights are optional.

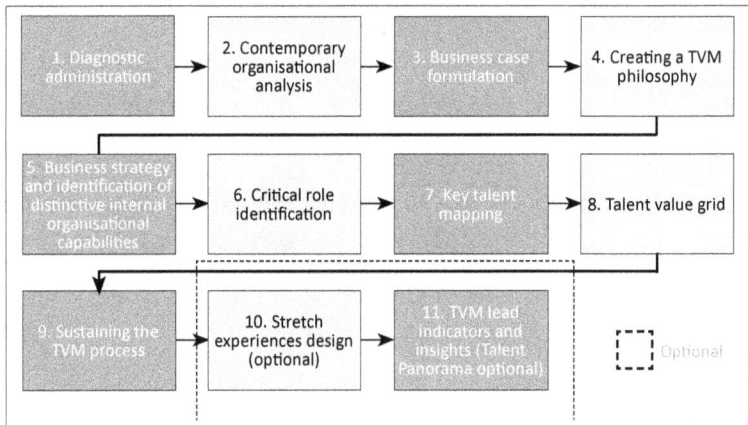

Figure 16: TVM Implementation process

Note: *the first nine steps are core to the implementation of TVM. Steps ten and eleven are optional implementation steps. In addition, the pre-implementation steps are not included as they form part of the influencing (change) plan – however, detail regarding the on-boarding is provided below.*

Figure 16 above will be used as a basic guide for this chapter.

The chapter will be split into several parts namely:

A.   **Pre – TVM deployment preparation**

This part discusses what data is required pre-deployment, the implementation project plan and the influencing plan

B.   **The TVM Implementation steps**

Steps 1 to 3

- Diagnostic Administration

- Contemporary organisational analysis

- Creating the business case

Step 4 - Creating the TVM philosophy

Steps 5 to 8 - Creating the TVG (See chapter 4)

Step 9 - Sustaining TVM

Steps 10 and 11 - Optional items

- Stretch Experiences (see chapter 12)

- Talent Insights (see chapter 13)

A.   Pre – TVM deployment preparation

Organisations can be introduced to TVM in numerous ways, for example:

1.   One or more of the CHRO, Chief Talent Officer, a member of the HR Team or CEO will read this book and try to implement it.

2.   The CEO, CHRO or Chief Talent Officer will receive basic information via social media pertaining to TVM and will attempt to reach subject matter experts on the subject to gain more insight.

3.   Certain stakeholders will attend a short session by a TVM specialist and will reach out to the guest speaker for more information.

4.   It is introduced to the CEO or CHRO by an external TVM subject matter expert.

Depending on who was first introduced to TVM in an organisation, the ease of deployment will differ. If the CEO was the first person who was introduced to TVM and has immediate buy-in to the concept and process, then it is normally easier to implement as the CEO can be considered to be the sponsor.

Alternatively, if the CHRO introduces TVM to the organisation then, depending on the CHRO's influence and standing in the organisation, it might not be as easy to implement it as when the CEO is sponsor. However, good CHROs know how to influence the right stakeholders especially if they are commercially astute.

TVM Introduction to the CEO

A high level view of TVM and its impact on business outcomes should be presented to the CEO. Ideally, the start of the discussion should revolve around how much additional profit the TVM process can deliver for the organisation. When pitching TVM to a CEO I will use the following phrase – "do you want your Key Talents to drive more value for the company?" This alludes to driving more profit. The CEO will want to know what the "size of the prize" is.

Very few CEO's will say no to the question, it normally solicits curiosity regarding TVM.

The pitch to the CEO should be crisp, succinct and short! The challenge that most HR Professionals have in a session with the CEO is that they too often revert to HR "language" which at times is perceived as theoretical or complex. Note: the purpose of the session with the CEO is not to ask permission to implement TVM but to ask for support. Talent Management will already be an institutionalised practice which will now be further enhanced.

A tactful HR Professional will build on the current business agenda to implement TVM. For example, in a FMCG company the CEO was very passionate and articulate about "Organisational Capabilities" and together with the Senior Leadership Team had identified 8 "Organisational Capabilities". If these exist in an organisation and are a key strategic focus, then approximately 30% of TVM is already implemented. HR will now need to leverage what exists by aligning the Key Talent to these "Organisational Capabilities" and agree specific business outcomes.

The most challenging way to introduce TVM is through a HR Function that has low legitimacy and a history of failing to implement business aligned solutions.

Regardless of how and by whom TVM was introduced into the organisation, the CHRO has the core role in implementing TVM successfully and hence a large part of the pre-deployment preparation will be done by the CHRO.

Preparation will require that the CHRO gather base data before on-boarding and implementation starts. The base data will include:

1. The Strategic Plan of the company including the financial plan (the Profit and Loss Statement is the most important financial document)

2. Distinctive Internal Organisational Capabilities – these can normally be found in a company's mid-year or year-end reports. If a company does not know what its DIOCs are, then a DIOC identification process as part of TVM has to be instituted with key stakeholders (normally Departmental Heads) to determine what they are.

3. An estimate of what the current Talent Management programme is costing the company.

4. An estimate of what value can be derived by implementing TVM (additional guidance is provided later regarding the CFO's role in determining the estimate).

5. The current Talent Pool and how it is segmented.

6. The contemporary Talent Management process.

The CHRO will need this data to craft a basic "story" on what TVM is all about and why the organisation should be using it. A slide deck consisting of eight to ten slides should be used which incorporates the TVM philosophy as a compelling argument to implement TVM. The pre-TVM implementation slide deck should be used to influence both the CEO and CFO. Note: some of this information will be included in the Business Case.

Included in this slide deck should be a basic project and influencing plan.

B. TVM Implementation Steps

Steps 1 to 3 - Diagnosing

a. Diagnostic Administration

b. Contemporary organisational analysis

c. Creating the business case.

a. *Administering the TVM Diagnostic*

To assist companies in measuring the extent to which they are doing some of the TVM activities (HR Professionals generally understand parts of the Talent Management process as they might be currently doing some of the activities, but not the logical process) a diagnostic has been designed – (see Appendix 1). Figure 17 below is a sample of the diagnostic.

Business stakeholder alignment	Status
CEO, CFO, CHRO aligned on talent costs (Talent Valuation)	Meets standard
Talent Value Management understood by key stakeholders	Exceptional
Stakeholder commitment to TVM	Meets standard
HR community understand Talent Value Management	Exceptional
Key talent take accountability for achieving business outcomes	Meets standard
A TVM philosophy exists	Gap/risk
Distinctive Internal Organisation Capabilities (DIOC)	**Status**
Common understanding on Distinctive Internal Organisational Capabilities	Meets standard
DIOC have been identified	Meets standard
The DIOC have been prioritised and agreed	Meets standard
There is a clear link between the DIOC and the business imperatives/outcomes	Meets standard

Figure 17 – TVM Diagnostic

This diagnostic can be used in multiple ways:

1. To get an indication of what is currently being done or not being done.

2. To serve as course direction when implementing TVM.

3. To ascertain the progress that has been made after a certain period of TVM implementation.

The HR team should complete the diagnostic as some of the questions are HR related and require a deep understanding of the HR terminology. It can be administered at an individual level where each key HR Professional completes it independently and sends the completed instrument to a person who will collate and interpret the results. Alternatively, it can be done as a team with an independent facilitator.

65

Once the results are known, the HR Team will use this as a base to re-engineer the current Talent Management process. Note: re- engineering means that the activities are focused toward ensuring that the Key Talents achieve the business outcomes.

b.   Contemporary Organisation Analysis – the Current Reality – How much Talent Administration is being done

It is crucial that for TVM to be successful, the HR Team will need to increase its efficiency and re-direct its focus on some of the current Talent Management activities that they are performing.

Note: I reinforce the point once again – implementing TVM does not mean eliminating current Talent Management activities but rather ensuring that it all leads to a common purpose – ensuring the Talents add value. Therefore, it will be a refine, realignment, refocusing and in some cases elimination of non-value add Talent Activities. The Talent Admin Review List can be used to determine the extent to which Talent administration is being done.

The combination of administering a TVM diagnostic together with an assessment of current reality will form the basis for the shift to TVM.

c.   Creating the business case

The following data will be used to formulate a fact based business case on why the organisation needs to implement TVM:

1.   The pre- deployment information gathered as part of the "story" that was created about TVM.

2.   Insights from the diagnostic that was administered.

3.   A list of opportunities to reduce Talent administration identified through the Talent Admin Review list.

The business case should if possible contain data on the current spend on Talent Management within the organisation. The section below expands on the cost gathering exercise.

Costs Associated with running the Talent Function

So what does our current Talent Management programme cost us?

Below is a typical list of expenses associated with running a Talent Management Programme

Note: *these are not all the Talent costs, just the most obvious – there are many other indirect costs e.g. the cost of an IT system to record employee data and senior leaders' time invested in making Talent decisions:*

1. The compensation and benefits of the person who oversees the Talent role (in some instances this might be part of a multiple role);

2. Cost of conducting psychometric assessments;

3. Training and Development programme costs;

4. Mentoring and coaching costs;

5. Retention programmes costs;

6. The compensation and benefits of the Talents.

When added up, it is a significant number. It is crucial that HR have an indication, even if it is a rough estimate of what it currently costs, as HR will have to illustrate as a TVM outcome how much value was created through the focused TVM activities.

Imagine the level of increased legitimacy that the HR Function would have if it could demonstrate that the TVM process delivered a return of 10 times or more versus the actual costs – this can be achieved!

The business case, aimed at key stakeholders as the audience, should contain the following:

1. Brief Introduction to TVM.

2. What the current programme is costing.

3. Why TVM will create an increased ROI.

4. Information on what the business strategic imperatives are.

5. What the current year business targets are – focused on the 4 outcomes.

6. Draft DIOCs.

7. Example of a TVG.

8. What will change in the way that Talent Management is being done.

9. Draft project plan.

10. What resources would be required to deploy TVM.

11. Draft stakeholder influence plan.

Step 4 - Creating the TVM Philosophy

The creation of the business case will lay the platform for the formation of the Talent Philosophy. The concept of having a philosophy to underpin why and organisation does Talent Management was discussed in an earlier chapter. Many companies operate without a Talent Philosophy so it is not critical to success, but it does provide the organisation and all its employees with a context of why they do Talent Management.

Some companies have designed policies and procedures that govern the way that they do Talent Management. In most cases the dialogue focuses on building the pipeline, succession management and occasionally on having talent to drive the business strategy – all important reasons for doing Talent Management.

Implementing TVM will indeed require a review of current processes, policies and governance around Talent Management – but starting with a basic philosophy – **Talents should add higher value than the average employee.** Ideally this value is measured and monitored and is underpinned with robust, focused activities that support the Key Talents in achieving the value.

The essence of the Talent philosophy should always be centred around business outcomes, even a statement like "we are building our talent pipeline" or we are "strengthening our bench strength" is somewhat dated.

Note: *The formulation of the organisation's Talent Philosophy is a significant opportunity to provide a diverse stakeholder group with an opportunity to not only co-formulate it but to give them detail on what TVM is all about. It is strongly recommended that the formulation be an inclusive process. This will accelerate the TVM buy-in.*

Steps 5 to 8 - Creating the TVG

Creating a TVG requires a certain number of stakeholders to be present in a discussion. Most likely the CEO, CFO, Functional and Business Heads will need to provide input. The process can be started in a one-on-one basis (my experience has shown that this is the easiest way) complemented with a plenary session where all stakeholders are present in one room. The process will need to map out the 7 columns as well as the 3 grids presented in chapter 4.

Note: *read Chapters 4, 5, 6 & 7 before creating a TVG.*

All stakeholders need to be aligned on the completed TVG.

It is recommended that a logical stepped process is introduced, for example:

1. Start with the business outcomes that flow from the strategic imperatives;

2. Link the DIOCs to the business outcomes;

3. Link the DIOCs to the Critical Roles;

4. Align the Talent to the Critical roles.

Step 9 - Sustaining TVM – routines and processes

For TVM not to be a fad it has to institutionalised in the business. This means that the process of business outcomes identification and Key Talent alignment has to be done on an annual basis together with other processes, for example the ongoing identification of what DIOCs the company might need. Chapter 11 will provide the detail on how to sustain TVM.

Steps 10 and 11 - Optional items to implement

Stretch experiences and Talent indicators were discussed in Chapter 2 and will form part of Chapters 12 and 13. These are called optional as an organisation can chose to complement the TVM roll- out with these additional "value adds".

9

STAKEHOLDERS AND THEIR ROLES:
Who does what and why

Executive summary: For TVM to succeed, a large cohort of stakeholders will need to be involved in its implementation, in particular the Chief Executive Officer and Chief Financial Officer. Stakeholder roles and accountabilities for implementation and sustaining TVM have to be clear. The HR Function is the initial architect, change agent and most importantly the enabler of TVM through its support for the Key Talents.

In a meeting with a HR Leader of a major organisation, I provided him with insights on what some of the activities are that the Talent Manager had to perform as part of TVM. He soon realised that implementing TVM required the Talent Manager to shift his focus by at least 30% to activities that added value instead of the traditional *"maintenance of Talent spreadsheets"*. For emphasis, I provided him with examples of the type of TVM activities that I was engaged in during my tenure at some of the companies that I worked for – specifically the amount of time that I set aside to get closer to supporting Key Talent to drive value.

As TVM is such a new concept and a way of doing work, this chapter will explore some of the detail pertaining to the implementation activities that key stakeholders should be engaging in.

Special emphasis will be given to important role players in the Human Resources Function who have the largest responsibility to manage TVM. The TVM diagnostic in Appendix 1 gives some indication of what activities need to be executed.

The key Stakeholders

For TVM to be implemented successfully, it has to be seen as a **business initiative** supported by a progressive Human Resources intervention. The stakeholder cohort has to be as all-encompassing as possible as TVM will impact a large number of role holders in the organisation. It is important that these stakeholders have a deep orientation on what TVM means and the specific role that they will need to adopt to ensure its success.

Each stakeholder's role will be discussed in detail followed by a deep dive on the role that the HR team will need to fulfil. These stakeholders are:

1.   The Chief Executive Officer;

2.   Chief Financial Officer;

3.   Chief Marketing Officer;

4.   Business unit heads;

5.   Functional heads;

6.   Immediate manager; and the

7.   Key Talents.

The types of stakeholders that will need to be engaged might differ by organisation and nature of business, for example, the stakeholder cohort in a bank might be different from that in a mining company. Ultimately the Board or Senior Leadership team are the owners of TVM.

The Triad

The most important stakeholders are the CEO, CFO and the CHRO, or the triad. These three are the main sponsors of TVM. Early alignment amongst the three individuals on why the organisation needs to implement TVM and what the benefits are will ensure that its implementation gets off to a good start.

As TVM has a business slant, it is important that the process starts with the correct stakeholders. The CEO and CFO will have a vested interest on the outcomes of TVM and the CFO will be required to provide guidance and input to the company's financial outcomes so it is imperative that he or she forms part the initial on-boarding syndicate.

The CEO

Depending on the organisation design, the business leader (CEO, MD or Business Unit Head) has a key sponsor and advocacy role. This is the first person who needs to understand, support and provide resources for the implementation of TVM. Each of the roles is detailed below:

1. Sponsor

a. Approves the implementation of TVM;

b. Provides financial and human resources for the project;

c. Provides insight, context and perspective on the roll-out progress;

d. Ensures that there is organisational alignment at a senior leader level on the outcomes that need to be achieved;

e. Influences senior leaders to realise the business outcomes that the Key Talent will achieve.

2. Advocacy

a. Encourages the organisation to adopt TVM;

b. Becomes an active change agent to ensure that TVM is implemented and sustained.

The Chief Financial Officer

Most experienced CFOs, when requested to provide guidance and data to the HR Function on how the HR Function can support the organisation to increase profitability or market share, will willingly put time aside to play this role. It is not often that the HR Function has a business discussion with the Finance Function and it normally comes as a pleasant engagement with HR. The CFO has a similar sponsor and advocacy role as the CEO, the primary differences being:

1. *Providing finance data (normally the Marketing function will have the market share data)*

a. The CFO will provide data on what the key upcoming financial opportunities are that the TVM process can assist in achieving. He/she can identify what the financial targets are as well as the risks associated with achieving it. For example, he/she can indicate that the revenue target is ten percent growth on prior year and that the main risk is that consumers might not respond to the increase in price of certain products that will partly drive this ten percent growth.

b. Updates on progress against key business outcome targets.

c. In addition, the CFO will provide a realistic view of what can be achieved by a Key Talent. (Note that this quantification of potential achievement by a Key Talent needs to be aligned with the individual's line leader).

2. *Guidance on DIOC /Business Outcome Alignment*

a. Once the DIOCs have been agreed by the organisation, the CFO will have an important role in aligning them to the business outcomes. Each of the identified DIOCs has to align with one or several of the business outcomes, either revenue, margins, cost reduction, or market share.

b. The CFO will also be an important contributor to the initial identification of the DIOCs.

Chief Marketing Officer (CMO)

The involvement of the CMO will depend on the type and nature of the organisation involved in implementing TVM. The CMO will provide data on the overall market share as well as the different portfolio and product market shares. In many FMCG organisations, the Sales as well as the Marketing heads will provide relevant data pertaining to actual as well as planned market share (it is important that the Sales head agrees to the market share aspirations).

In addition, he /she can be a valuable contributor to the identification of DIOCs

Business Unit heads

This is once again dependent on the nature of the organisation and its design. It will be important for all business unit heads to have a good understanding of TVM as their role, like the CEOs will be advocacy and support. In addition, they will be required to show how their Key Talents are achieving the agreed business outcomes. They, together with the immediate manager, will have a vested interest in the Key Talent's success as it is directly linked to their unit's success.

Functional Heads

These are important stakeholders as the Key Talents will be representative of their specific areas – depending on which DIOCs are agreed and prioritised. For example, the Head of Information Technology might not play a direct role in selecting a Key Talent to drive a DIOC if the DIOC is not related to the Information Technology Function. However, if he/she is part of the Senior Leadership Team, then advocacy will be an important role.

Immediate Manager

These are the individuals who can either accelerate or decelerate the implementation of TVM. If they do not see it as the way that the organisation manages talent, but rather as a cumbersome duty which distracts them from achieving their objectives, then implementing TVM will be a major challenge. They have to believe that it will add value to them and their respective units and that it is a natural way of achieving results. Ultimately their role is to own TVM.

The line leader together with HR will have the following roles:

a. Support and continuously motivate the Key Talent as he/she attempts to achieve the business outcomes.

b. Provide or request resources to achieve the business outcomes.

c. Be the coach during the TVM implementation phase to the Key Talent and the rest of his/her team.

d. Identify knowledge and skills gaps that the Key Talent might have in achieving the business outcomes.

e. Assist with the closing of the Key Talent's knowledge and skills gaps.

Key Talents

These are the individuals who carry the greatest contribution and personal risk in achieving the business outcomes. As a cohort they have been identified as having the potential to drive significant organisational value and will therefore receive more visibility and attention from the Senior Leadership team. Other Talents will also have *some* contribution and risk profile – however, Key Talents are singled out as they have a larger proportion of value to add.

Risk comes in the form of possible failure – however the organisation has to accept this risk and not translate it into career risk for the Key Talent. *Hence it is critical that the right Talents are selected to drive outcomes and receive organisational support at all levels.*

The Key Talents have several roles to play:

a. Ensure that they have a deep understanding of TVM and the company's expectations;

b. Provide updates on progress on achievement of the business outcomes;

c. Identify any de-railers or risks in the achievement of the business outcomes;

d. Request support and guidance;

e. Achieve the designated business outcome.

The HR Role

In this section I will cover several areas where HR will play a key role in embedding TVM. This section will be segmented into several parts namely:

a. Prerequisites for successful HR implementation.

b. Introducing, implementing and sustaining TVM.

c. Alignment sessions.

a. Prerequisites for successful HR implementation

There are several prerequisites for HR to implement and sustain TVM – note these are not in any particular order:

1. *Breaking out of the Talent Administration mode – mentally and physically.*

It seems that administration and compliance is a comfort zone for HR Professionals, the paradox being that most progressive HR Professionals have a deep yearning to engage in more transformational type work. Either they feel trapped in their current routines or they just don't have a good understanding of how to shift the emphasis to more value add activities. Even more challenging is the organisational view that HR should be doing administration duties, ensure compliance to policies or solve people problems which line leaders should have initially resolved.

In some countries, depending on the labour legislative framework, HR will be expected to have a more extensive administrative role. However, this does not mean that administration should be the alpha and omega of what HR should be doing.

TVM will allow the HR Function to seriously re-think how it currently performs its roles – particularly if the Function and its activities are a repetition of the last fifteen to twenty years and are inwardly focused with very little business value.

In the last two to three years I have seen a significant amount of debate and progressive thinking on what the HR Function should be doing. A lot of this thinking on business aligned HR functions will be deployed in the next two to five years meaning that many HR Functions will be restructured around how best to add value.

2. Understand TVM – beyond a conceptual level

TVM affords the HR Professionals the opportunity to think very deeply on how they do Talent Management – but from a business perspective. It can take a while for the HR Professionals to truly understand TVM.

The HR Professionals must have a collective and thorough understanding of TVM as they will be expected to play multiple roles in its implementation. For example, the development of Key Talents will be much more focused on enabling them to add the business value.

Experience has shown that, even if TVM is implemented, it takes a few months for HR Professionals to truly understand its impact on the way that they do Talent Management. They first have to "unfreeze" the way they currently view Talent Management.

TVM disrupts the way that they are currently doing Talent Management hence a psychological discomfort normally manifests itself at the introduction of the concept. However once they understand and commence implementation, it becomes a "breath of fresh air".

3.   Being Commercially Astute

The HR Professionals will need to accelerate their understanding of the business and its key drivers, particularly how the company makes money. In addition, they will need a very good understanding of what DIOCs are conceptually and in their own organisation.

If they find reading and understanding the Profit and Loss Statement a challenge, then it will be difficult for them to map the Key Talent to business outcomes. TVM assumes that they have a certain amount of commercial astuteness and if this is currently at a low level amongst the HR Professionals, TVM will certainly assist them to to improve as they implement it.

In addition, HR Professionals must have a good idea of how the company works, how it makes, markets, sells and distributes its products – having a good understanding of the organisation's value chain.

4.   Influencing key stakeholders

As this process involves a significant number of stakeholders, some degree of change management is required from a macro organisational level to a micro individual level. This will indeed require some communication, alignment, education – or in its broader sense an influencing plan.

b.   HR's role in introducing, implementation and sustaining TVM

CHRO – crafting the story

The CHRO will be responsible for formulating the basic "story" on TVM. This influencing document will be used to on-board key stakeholders. In addition, the CHRO will own the implementation plan.

CHRO and Chief Talent Officer

The CHRO together with the Chief Talent officer will need to design a conceptual presentation regarding the business case for TVM. This conceptual view should not contain too much information but more the essence of what it is all about and how it can add significant value to the organisation. The document should contain information on the concepts, definitions and basic implementation process. It is important that there is clarity on how much value it can add to the company as well as detail on what TVM is versus current Talent practices. The aim is to reinforce that current practices are *not* eliminated but refined, refocused and complemented with additional processes which are more business aligned, for example, alignment of Key Talents with DIOCs and business outcomes. See chapter 9 for more detail on the Business Case formulation.

CHRO, Chief Talent Officer and CFO

The meeting with the CFO will be important for a number of reasons other than for obtaining buy- in. The purpose of the session is to obtain information on DIOCs, Critical Roles and business outcomes.

The same conceptual slides designed above will be used as an introduction to TVM, particularly the segment on the TVM process and the concept of DIOCs, Critical roles and Key Talent alignment. Showing the CFO a mock up version of the Talent Value Grid will be a good idea.

The first question for the CFO should centre around the business results for the current year or for the planned year (the question will depend on how far the organisation is with its current financial year). Of particular interest will be the revenue, gross margin, and cost reduction targets (the CFO might have an idea on market share but the conversation with the Chief Marketing Officer will carry more credibility).

The second question will be about what the CFO believes are the DIOCs that will drive the achievement of the business results. Note: the CFO will give an opinion on what the DIOCs could be – these will be ratified by each of the functional heads.

The third question will be about the Critical Roles in the organisation that drive the DIOCs.

This meeting should culminate in a clear idea of what the possible business outcomes are, the Critical Roles and the DIOCs.

CHRO, Chief Talent Officer and Chief Marketing Officer

The outcome of this session is agreement on what the market share targets are for the company. Depending on the product or service portfolio, there might be several market share targets. However, it is best recorded at an aggregate level, for example, what the overall market share of the company should be for a certain product or service category (for example, the market shares for carbonated soft drinks). When the DIOC, Critical Roles, Key Talent and business alignment session takes place, it will be better to have the market shares fragmented into various products. So it is important to obtain as much information as possible.

The Chief Marketing Officer will, depending on whether any of the DIOCs are in the Marketing area, identify Critical roles for the function.

TVM introduction to the HR Team

At this stage the following will exist in terms of a business case for TVM:

1. A conceptual view of the TVM philosophy, concepts and key processes.
2. Information on the business outcomes that can be achieved as well as the DIOCs.
3. A broad project plan.

4. A stakeholder influencing map which includes a basic communication plan.

5. Resources that might be required.

6. Basic information on what will and what will not change in the current Talent Management practices.

There is now sufficient information to present to the HR Team. During this session the HR team will get a very good *intellectual* understanding of TVM and will have a chance to interrogate the overall thinking, particularly if there will be any implications for the recruitment, assessment, learning and development, compensation and other HR activities. Below is an example of what HR activities could possibly be refined and refocused:

1. Talent Management process change – a process that now starts with the business outcomes and ends with the ratification of Key Talents versus a process which starts with a Talent name list.

2. Assessing Key Talents against the ability to build, refine or maintain the DIOC and deliver the business outcomes instead of broad generic assessment.

3. Highly customised learning and development interventions which accelerate the growth of the Key Talents instead of generic collective learning and development interventions.

The outcome of this session with the HR team is overall understanding of TVM as well as buy-in. Note: see the **From and To Chart** in Figure 18 below for more detail to provide to the HR team.

From	To
A generic Talent Philosophy	A short concise business aligned philosophy
Talent Administration	An integrated Talent Value Management process

From	To
A repetitive process with multiple outcomes and indicators	A clear process with defined business outcomes
Poorly aligned Talent to business outcomes	Key Talent aligned to business outcomes
Focus on a large Talent pool	Focus on a Key Talent cohort
HR driven process	Business driven process
Passive Talent Management	Pro-active reverse engineered Talent Value Management
Chief Talent Officer centric Talent activities	Talent activities centred around Key Talent enablement and business outcomes

Figure 18: From Talent Administration to Talent Value Management

10

TVM ROUTINES

Executive Summary: The Talent agenda requires that an organisation have a certain "talent rhythm" with specific routines and processes. The key challenge is to make those routines as productive and as value add as possible. Most routines are purposeful and planned, however, some might be unplanned and would be dependent on when a specific event occurs for example, conducting psychometric assessment and other forms of assessment on the Key Talent. Once TVM is implemented, these routines are key to sustaining it.

Annual Talent Value Grid (TVG)

The most important routine is the annual creation of the TVG. This document/tool requires dedicated time to formulate it. It is recommended that the TVG be compiled annually or when there has been a change, for example a Key Talent leaves the organisation or is promoted to another role.

All the stakeholders discussed in the previous section of the book will be involved in its compilation and ratification.

Ratification will take place at a formal meeting with all the important stakeholders being present – Senior Leadership Team/ Functional and Business Unit heads.

Note: *if there are additional DIOCs that the organisation would like to build during the year, this might mean a change to the Key Talent on the list, and therefore the TVG will change.*

Identification of stretch experiences

As an outflow of the TVG ratification session, it would be expedient if organisations had a robust dialogue on what the Stretch Experiences would be for each of the Key Talent. I suggest that this happens at the same time as the review of the annual TVG. Stretch Experiences could be expensive and thus it is important that the right stakeholder group is present to approve the necessary resources.

Quarterly review of progress

It is recommended that the TVG be reviewed quarterly for 2 purposes:

1. Assessing progress against the agreed business outcomes by the Key Talents.

2. Assessing what support the Key Talents would require to achieve the business outcomes.

On-boarding of new stakeholders

As the stakeholder group changes within the organisation (for example somebody being transferred or promoted), these new stakeholders will need to be given an orientation on what TVM is all about and their respective roles and accountabilities

SECTION 4

TVM ACCELERATORS

INTRODUCTION

TVM accelerators refer to certain additional activities,requirements and practices that enhance and accelerate its implementation. They are not essential for success and might not be core to the TVM process but they will make a difference.
There are three important accelerators namely:

1.   Commercial astuteness for HR.

2.   Stretch Experiences for Key Talents.

3.   Talent Insights – TVM lead indicators.

There could be many more, for example, culture can be an accelerator - in an organisation culture that is open to change, TVM will be implemented more quickly than in a culture where change resistance is high.

The three accelerators laws are mutually exclusive, the one is not dependent on the other.

Chapter 11 will cover commercial astuteness for HR and why it is important for the HR team to be business savvy. TVM has a business orientation and requires that the HR team can relate to key business concepts and processes. Poor commercial astuteness might inhibit smooth implementation.

Chapter 12 will explore the concept of Stretch Experiences for Key Talents particularly how the right development can help build DIOCs.

Chapter 13 will look at Talent Insights (or metrics) which are aligned to TVM.

11

COMMERCIAL ASTUTENESS FOR HR:
Understanding what the business requires

Executive Summary: Commercial astuteness is a fairly new way of describing an important competency for the HR team – not only for TVM purposes but to ensure that they formulate and deploy business aligned HR interventions. Building commercial astuteness is not a once off intervention but a life- long journey for all HR Professionals. Being commercially astute involves constant vigilance and mental alertness to identify opportunities to advance the business agenda with the right people solutions.

? *So what is Commercial Astuteness?*

> My definition of commercial astuteness is "Being knowledgeable and mentally alert to the way that a business operates in order to identify opportunities to add value through impactful HR interventions".

The definition is broader than that of commercial or business acumen – which normally focuses on the key business and financial concepts and processes that HR should be aware of – "acumen" seems to be more about understanding whereas "astuteness" is a call to action.

Commercial astuteness is a much more dynamic concept and requires constant vigilance and mental alertness as to what the present and future business challenges are on a daily basis and being immersed in understanding what they mean. For example, here are some key questions that involve commercial astuteness:

1. How is our market share versus the competitors, why are they gaining share,do we lack an innovative product pipeline?

2. The latest product launch – has it been successful?

3. The digital marketing strategy – what resources and know-how do we need?

4. The distribution efficiency of the company – how can we reduce the cost of distribution?

5. How can we get our products to a new class of consumer?

6. How do we grow our revenue, is it price or volume driven?

All these organisational dynamics have a human dynamic element embedded in them – the secret and skill is to identify what they are. For example, how digital savvy is the Marketing team and what skills and knowledge would they require to be best in class?

Figure 19 below shows a framework called the Human Insights HR Legitimacy Ladder. The framework serves as a guide for self-development for HR professionals. It contains focus areas which HR Professionals need to master to increase their impact. For more information on the HR Legitimacy Ladder read the article that appeared in the Human Capital Review. Article link below :(http://www.humancapitalreview.org/content/default.asp?Article_ID=1514)

To implement TVM, HR Professionals will need to increase their commercial astuteness. This will also enable a more strategic view of their work generally (notice that commercial astuteness lies towards the strategic domain on the ladder).

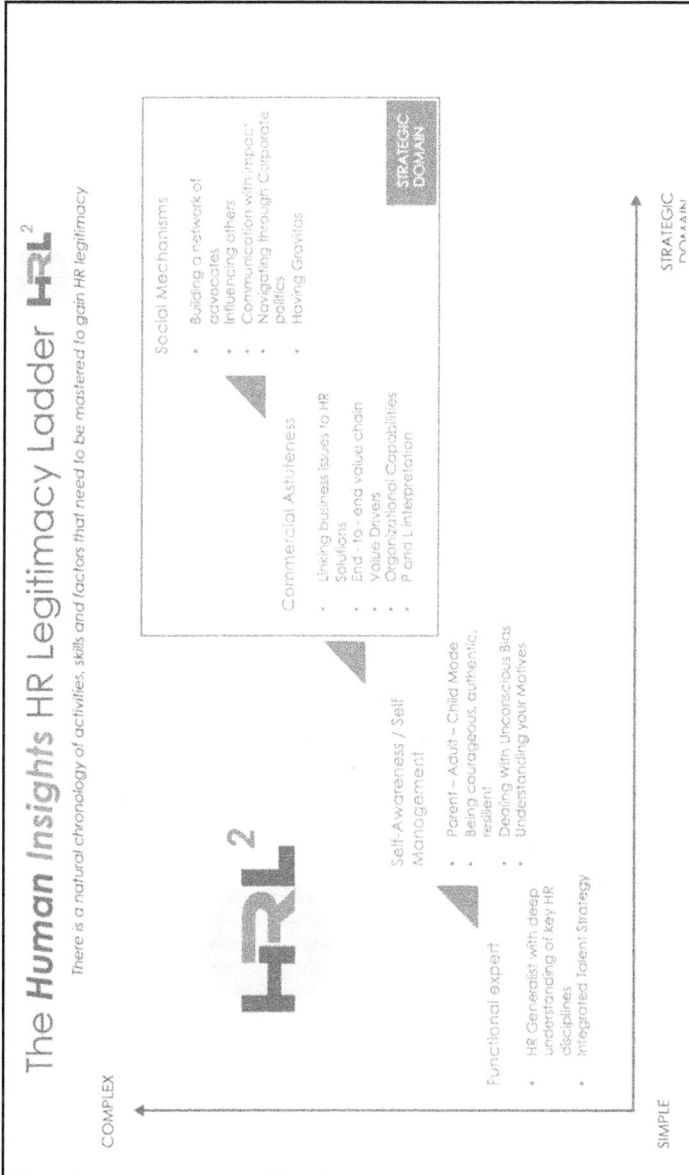

Figure 19 – The HR Legitimacy Ladder

There is consensus amongst HR Professionals that commercial astuteness is normally acquired later in one's career and not earlier – even if the person has a commercial qualification. Drawing the link between a business issue and the people dynamics that emanate from it is not easy. The case study below will illustrate that not even CEO's can easily draw this link:

> I worked as a HR Executive for a Beverage company which increased the price of its premium brand to be significantly higher than its competitors on an annual basis. This happened over a three-year period. The CEO believed that being the market leader in the specific category gave the company the "authority" to hike prices which he believed was sustainable. So instead of driving volume to increase revenue, prices were increased and made the revenue line look good. However, there was a problem with this business strategy which had a direct HR implication. The problem was that volumes were flat, and to aggravate the situation, significant capital investments were made for new machinery which could significantly increase output – but volumes were not increasing. The HR implication of the business decision was that the factories became inefficient and did not have long production runs that were needed to keep production costs low. Ultimately, the company had to reduce headcount through a downsizing exercise as profits were declining year on year. The inefficiencies and people implications were pointed out to the CEO, whose solution was to employ an Industrial Engineer to solve the problem in the factories – but this was not where the problem was.

There should be a constant conscious alertness by HR Professionals to keep track of what the business challenges are. Thus the question that should be continuously asked is:

? *What are the HR implications of what is happening in the business!*

Quite often HR Professionals will ask me how they could improve their commercial astuteness – not an easy question to answer. The challenge starts the way which HR is being taught at academic institutions – Human Sciences and Business Sciences need a deeper integrated approach. For example, how does one help HR Professionals relate to value chains in the Business Science area and link this to Human Science challenges within the value chain.

STRETCH EXPERIENCES:
Growing talent in an irreversible way

Executive Summary: Stretch experiences are planned, purposeful development of Key Talents in a way that takes them out of their comfort zone and results in irreversible growth. Ideally, the development opportunity is linked to the building or enhancement of a DIOC. Stretch experiences develop both behavioural and technical skills.

What are stretch experiences?

My simple explanation of stretch experiences relates to those development opportunities that create irreversible growth for the individual – the person is never the same after the intervention. My best personal development always occurred when I was placed in a challenging situation over a prolonged period (for a few months). Here are a few examples of stretch experiences:

1.   Leading a project to form a new organisational unit with a team of highly capable individuals.

2.   Being placed in a new role in a country where the culture of the country and the way that work was done was different from what you have previously experienced.

3.   Leading a different function from one in which you have been in before, for example the Head of HR leading a Marketing Function.

In the examples above, learning is accelerated for both behavioural and technical (functional) skills.

Features of stretch experiences

Stretch experiences can be characterised by the following:

1. Acceleration of an individual's ability.

2. They take the individual outside his/her comfort zone.

3. They occur mostly on-the-job.

4. Both technical and behavioural skills are acquired.

5. They are normally complex and challenging.

6. They involve some form of career risk for the individual.

7. They develop multiple skills at the same time.

8. They are not normally short in duration.

Talent Development – the current challenge

Most organisations will use a combination of development interventions to "upskill" their Talents. These interventions might include (amongst others):

1. Formal in- house classroom based training and development.

2. External training and development at a Business School or specialist Learning and Development Institute.

3. On-the -job training and development.

4. Coaching and/or mentoring.

My experience has shown that many of these interventions have a marginal impact on the organisation's results. The link to the learning event and application to drive business outcomes is in most instances non-existent. Even more challenging is the fact that very little transfer of knowledge and skill actually takes place and is applied back at work. The problem of misdiagnosed and low impact learning and development interventions lies in:

1. The degree to which the learning and development need is accurately identified; and

2. The type of development intervention that is prescribed to close the knowledge/skill gap.

TVM has a practical and a powerful way of aligning Key Talent to DIOCs and business outcomes which creates the platform to accurately identify the development need and the "Stretch Experience" to close the gap.

How to build DIOCs through stretch experiences

A DIOC consists of a multitude of items (levers) and working with these provides a Key Talent a unique opportunity to build the DIOC and at the same time increase his/her personal proficiency.

For example, an organisation might have identified Centralised Procurement as a DIOC, and that the Key Talent to drive this DIOC would be an internal candidate who had the passion and technical proficiency to create the DIOC. The organisation will then identify which Stretch Experiences would be best for the Key Talent to build the DIOC. One such stretch experience could be a project that is given to the incumbent to review global best practices within the Centralised Procurement area. This project would take a few months and will not only stretch the person technically but behaviourally as well, for example project management skills could be developed.

The first step would be to identify those DIOCs that need to be built, enhanced or refined. I have used the grid below (Figure 20) many times over the last few years to identify the current strength of a DIOC within an organisation. Gap means that the DIOC is weak within the organisation, Build means that work to strengthen the DIOC has commenced and Strength means that the DIOC is a competitive advantage.

Once the organisation completes the necessary assessment of the DIOC, the next step is to identify the Key Talent who will be responsible for building it....in this way a stretch opportunity is identified.

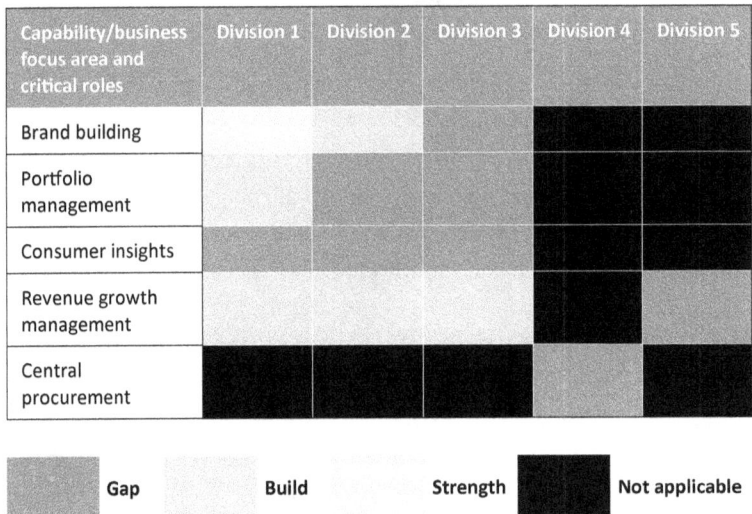

Capability/business focus area and critical roles	Division 1	Division 2	Division 3	Division 4	Division 5
Brand building					
Portfolio management					
Consumer insights					
Revenue growth management					
Central procurement					

Gap   Build   Strength   Not applicable

Figure 20 – DIOC Assessment chart

13

TALENT INSIGHTS

Executive Summary: *Talent metrics are important indicators for progress evaluation and monitoring. There are many possible metrics. Some of these metrics can indeed assist the organisation in making better fact based decisions. The key challenge will always be to identify those metrics which will drive the right discussion around value creation. Less is best, and having too many unrelated and poorly integrated metrics only ends up as more Talent Administration. TVM metrics are aligned to the TVM philosophy and are lead indicators that provide important information on how the Talent are progressing on achieving the business outcomes.*

Talent Lag versus Lead indicators

Lag Indicators

Lag indicators are those which provide a reactive view of the past. These indicators provide basic information on what has happened and in most cases they are a "nice to know" - for example what percentage of our Talents were recently promoted. This is just data which has no direct or indirect connection to a revenue line!

Lag indicators exist in many organisations which do not have a clear Talent Philosophy and Talent Strategy. Requests for Talent data are random and providing this data is an energy sapping exercise. Data formats, templates, and interpretation constantly change – depending on who requests the data.

There is very little link between business outcomes and the Talent metrics and in many instances there is very little consensus on what the actual metric measures and why it is important.

Examples of lag indicators:

1. Number of Talents attending external training programmes.

2. Percentage of the Learning and Development budget spent on Talents.

3. Racial and gender profile of Talents attending Learning and Development programmes.

4. Number of Talents assessed through psychometric assessments.

5. Percentage of Talents who have mentors.

Lead Indicators

These are proactive measures that provide deep insight to a specific issue that creates a call to action for the organisation. Unlike lag indicators they are linked to a very clear Talent programme purpose and strategy. Based on the data that these indicators provide, timeous and factual decisions can be made that will advance the business outcomes.

These lead indicators provide insight for business decision making.

Figure 21 below illustrates the process from data to business decision:

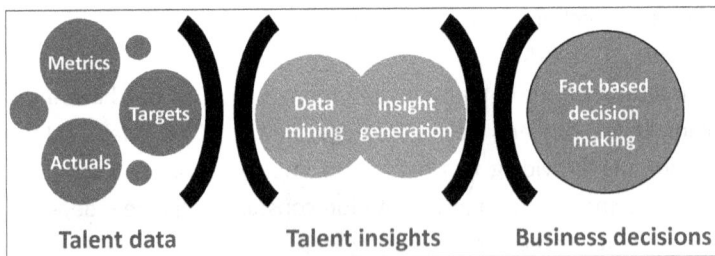

Figure 21 – From data to Business Insights process flow

Examples of TVM lead indicators

1. Percentage of Critical Roles filled by Key Talent

2. Percentage of Key Talent driving Distinctive Internal Organisational Capabilities

3. Percentage achievement of agreed business outcomes by Key Talents.

4. Percentage successors to Key Talents

Figure 22 below is a basic tool which can be used to record and track TVM lead indicators:

Indicator	Description	Target	Actual	Comments
% Talent in agreed critical roles	Percentage of the talent in a talent pool who are currently in a critical role that have been identified by the business	60%	55%	
% Talent driving distinctive internal organisation capabilities	Percentage of key talent proactively and purposeful placed in roles that drive agreed organisational capabilities			
% of development plans implemented	Percentage of talent with development plans that have been completed/actioned			
% of successors for talent in critical roles	Percentage talent in critical roles who have successors			Note: the readiness of the successors need to be agreed as this is a strong indicator of pipeline strength

Exceeds target   Meets target   Does not meet target

Figure 22 – Talent Lead Indicators Chart

SECTION 5

THE CALL TO ACTION

14

TVM – THE NEW NORMAL!

A changing world view of Talent Management

There seems to be change in momentum worldwide by progressive organisations to revise their current "outdated" approach to Talent Management. This change has been fuelled by the continuous questioning and challenges the HR function has faced regarding the value that it adds.

At the same time, organisations seem to have a more mature understanding of Organisation Capabilities. This creates a significant opportunity now to align Key Talent to the Organisation Capabilities in order to achieve certain business outcomes.

Business leaders are starting to challenge the HR assumptions on which contemporary Talent management are based. They are demanding a greater need for Talent to add value to the bottom line. Our challenge is how to complement what we have implemented over the last few years in an efficient and rational manner – we do not want to be seen as implementing another fad.

We have this window of opportunity to rethink and review what Talent Management means and present a different philosophy and approach to better align with the organisations objectives. Complacency and maintaining the status quo is not an option.

? What are the things that you can do immediately?

Challenge

Review and challenge the current assumptions on which your current Talent Management process is being executed. Start with an open mind and ask the question – if I had to start a Talent Management function from scratch, where would I start and what will I implement. Centre this interrogation around the key question – does this add value? Many Talent Management functions in today's organisations are based on outdated assumptions and processes – the strange thing is that most companies have a very similar model and process but this does not meet many organisations' needs.

Change your view – external versus internal

Get a global view of what progressive organisations are doing in Talent Management, and see what progress they have made in the last two to three years in aligning Talent to organisation value. Certain HR consulting organisations as well HR thought leaders are espousing a new view on Talent Management – the change momentum has started!

Get a deeper understanding of what drives your business

Crucial for TVM success is the need for HR to get a deeper understanding on how their organisations make money. The HR Professional's understanding of the business will need to go beyond a conceptual level to a real understanding of the value chain, key business and finance concepts and how all the functions work together to create value.

Less compliance and administrative focus

The compliance and administrative burden is a major hurdle for most HR Functions – more so in countries where there is an onerous labour legislative environment. The HR Team become highly proficient in compliance and administration and seem either to have too little time for the more value adding HR activities or they have not had a chance to learn how to apply the more complex HR transformational agenda. TVM presents the HR team an opportunity to see the world through a different lens and ensures that they do more than the energy sapping administrative and compliance activities.

Commence the dialogue on how HR can add value

The dialogue with the CEO and CFO regarding how HR can add value is guaranteed to be a liberating encounter for HR as well as the business. How better to be proactive and drive a much needed value add agenda!

Triple benefits

Implementing TVM provides multiple direct and indirect benefits for the organisation, the most significant being the realisation of value. However, in the process of realising this value the organisation gets the added benefit of building, refining or enhancing its current Organisational Capabilities. Lastly, HR has the opportunity to do work which they will find refreshing and challenging!

So become a TVM champion and realise those benefits today!

Appendix 1 (Sample)

Business stakeholder alignment	Status
CEO, CFO, CHRO aligned on talent costs (Talent Valuation)	Meets standard
Talent Value Management understood by key stakeholders	Exceptional
Stakeholder commitment to TVM	Meets standard
HR community understand Talent Value Management	Exceptional
Key talent take accountability for achieving business outcomes	Meets standard
A TVM philosophy exists	Gap/risk
Distinctive Internal Organisation Capabilities (DIOC)	
Common understanding on Distinctive Internal Organisational Capabilities	Meets standard
DIOC have been identified	Meets standard
The DIOC have been prioritised and agreed	Meets standard
There is a clear link between the DIOC and the business imperatives/outcomes	Meets standard
Critical roles	
Critical roles have been identified to drive the DIOC	Under development
Critical roles have been prioritised	
There is an aligned understanding of what critical roles are	Meets standard
A critical role/DIOC grid exists	
Key talent	

An aligned and ratified talent pool exists	Meets standard
The concept of key talent is understood	
Key talent have been identified	
Key talent in critical roles have been identified	Meets standard
Key talent in critical roles aligned to the DIOC exists	Meets standard
A key talent/critical role/DIOC grid exists	Meets standard
Key talent understand TVM	Meets standard
Talent value management	
Key talent are linked to critical roles/DIOC and business outcomes	Under development
A talent value grid exists	Gap/risk
Stretch experiences have been identified for key talent	Gap/risk
Quarterly meeting with key talent to review progress on stretch experiences	Under development
Development planning completed for key talent	Meets standard
Psychometric assessments planned with proactive remit to assessors	
Outcomes of psychometric assessments used to accelerate key talent achievement of business results	
TVM routines	
Annual TVM review by executive leadership	Meets standard
Quarterly review of the talent value grid at executive level	

Appendix 2

Talent Admin Review List

Activity	Build	Refine	Refocus	Eliminate
A Talent Philosophy exists				
A business aligned Talent strategy exists				
Criteria for Talent selection exist				
Talent selected according to agreed criteria				
Talent master list exists				
Performance/potential grid used				
Talent master list updated monthly				
Annual Talent Review occurs				
Quarterly review of Talent list and progress				
Quarterly Talent reviews conducted				
Business outcomes identified for Key Talent to achieve				
Talent Aligned To Distinctive Internal Organisational Capabilities				
Critical Roles identified				
A Talent Value Grid exists				

Activity	Build	Refine	Refocus	Eliminate
Assessment of Talent is based on a development philosophy				
Criteria for Talent assessment exists				
Psychometric assessments and other assessments conducted on Talent				
Talent assessment results aggregated and used to determine development needs				
Assessment reports are screened and key development needs identified				
Feedback post assessment provided to Talents				
Talent trained in development planning				
Training and Development is highly customized to meet individual needs				
Line leaders trained in Talent Management				
A clear Talent Training plan exists				
A process for identifying and ratifying stretch experiences exists				

Activity	Build	Refine	Refocus	Eliminate
Central co-ordination of all Talent Development				
Thirty percent of the Talent Manager's time is spent on Talent Development				
The Talent Manager has a very close relationship with Key Talents				
The Talent Manager's role and accountabilities are clearly defined				
Evaluation of Talent training occurs				
Clear succession plans are in place				
A Talent retention plan exists				
Talent metrics identified				
Talent metrics are business aligned				
Quarterly updating and review of Talent metrics				
Talent metrics used to gain insights for decision making				

Index

www.ingramcontent.com/pod-product-compliance
Lightning Source LLC
Chambersburg PA
CBHW071155200326
41519CB00018B/5242